'John Hull is always interesting, stimulating, and prepared to adopt unusual approaches. This is no less true of his latest book, which – by accessing the Bible through the sorts of reflections on and perceptions of blindness that have been part of his earlier writings – offers a unique perspective, with many inspirational and enticing insights.'
David Blunkett, MP, Secretary of State for Education and Employment

'A masterpiece . . . The observation is minute, and equally it is profound: everything is pondered, explored, to its limit – every experience turned this way and that, until it yields its full harvest of meanings. The incisiveness of Hull's observation, the beauty of his language, make this book poetry; the depth of his reflection turns it into phenomenology or philosophy.'
Oliver Sacks on Touching the Rock *in the* New York Review of Books

'The depth of John Hull's reflective theology does far more than take you into his own experience as a blind person; it takes you back into your own life if you are a sighted person to "see" it afresh; back into the scriptures with new "insight", and deeper into the heart of a God to whom darkness and light are both alike. This is a book that will speak to you and change you.'
Peter Selby, Bishop of Worcester

'This book deserves to be read by a wide public. When its author became blind in early middle age, he brought to the challenge of adjustment not only the strength of his Christian faith, but also the will to continue to pursue his chosen profession and, just as important, the ability to perceive and articulate the problems which blind people face. His brilliant analysis, showing the extent to which the Bible itself expresses the distinctive perception of the former, is matched by his success in emphasising God's insistence that the latter are valued members of the human race and are not cast out from it. John Hull is to be congratulated on producing a work which is highly erudite and at the same time eminently readable.'
John A. Wall, CBE, formerly Cha *National Institute for the Blind*

In the Beginning
There was Darkness

*A Blind Person's Conversations
with the Bible*

John M. Hull

scm press

ISBN 0 334 02821 3

First published 2001
by SCM Press
9–17 St Albans Place, London N1 0NX

SCM Press is a division of
SCM-Canterbury Press Ltd

Typeset at Rowland Phototypesetting,
Bury St Edmunds, Suffolk
Printed in Great Britain by
Biddles Ltd, Guildford and King's Lynn

To Marilyn

Contents

6 Blind Bible/blind God

7 Jesus

A word of thanks

I am grateful to a number of people who helped me in the writing of this book. Liz Potts, Julie Foster, Abby Sandor and John Hobby produced the printed text. Lee Differ, Liese Perrin and David Coppock got books from the library, helped with concordances, made coffee, looked things up in the Bible when work with cassettes was just too slow, checked the entire manuscript and were always good-humoured about it. Professor Emeritus Michael Goulder read the whole manuscript and made many helpful suggestions. I would also like to express my thanks to the St Peter's College Saltley Trust whose generous grant made possible the preparation of this work. Quotations from the Bible are from the New Revised Standard Version, unless otherwise indicated. I am especially grateful to Marilyn, whose face I have been unable to forget and who has sustained me in hope.

JMH
University of Birmingham, October 2000

Introduction

In the beginning there was darkness

'The earth was a formless void and darkness covered the face of the deep' (Gen. 1.2). The Bible begins with darkness and shapelessness, with the loss of form and with the experience of the abyss. Can I not say, as a blind person, that the Bible begins at the place where I now find myself? When you are in the dark, your surroundings lose their shape. As someone who has passed through the loss of sight, have I not experienced the shapelessness of the void? The first thing the Bible tells me about blindness is that there is a connection between it and the earliest creative presence of the Holy Spirit.

'Then God said: "Let there be light"' (v. 3). In this part of the Bible, we are not told that God was the creator of darkness. The darkness had priority; it was already there, the first fact to be acknowledged. Elsewhere, we learn that God also created the darkness (Isa. 45.7); what we learn here is that God created the light and separated it from the darkness.

For me, the loss of sight was also an experience of separation. There is a great divide between the world perceived by sighted people and that perceived by blind people. The two realms are separate. In Genesis, we might think at first that light, once created, would abolish the darkness, but this is not what happened; darkness found a place in the night, and the night was separated from the day – separated, but joined.

This is characteristic of the experience of blind people, for whom many separations in life are both sharp and blurred.

One is joined closely to the very people from whom one is separated so sharply. The distinction between day and night, the distinction upon which the whole of this poem of creation depends, has a different meaning for blind people. Day is separated from night by a cycle of activity and rest, not by a cycle of light and darkness.

'And God saw that the light was good' (Gen. 1.4). Now we know what we have suspected throughout this passage: God is not on the side of blind people. God pronounces as good something that means nothing to those who are totally blind, and that is a source of longing and frustration, perhaps even despair, for those who still have a little sight. Here we come upon one of the great stumbling blocks that the Bible places in the way of blind people. It speaks of values that, for them, cannot be values. It announces that God is on the side of, and has a preference for, a world that is not their world – a reality to which they have no access.

'God called the light Day, and the darkness he called Night' (v. 5). God calls it the night, and in naming it becomes its Lord and gives it a place. 'There was evening and there was morning, the first day' (v. 5). The day was made up of evening and morning, and included both darkness and light. The darkness is now equal to the light: each occupies half of the day. Moreover, the order is now reversed; although God first called the light day and only afterward called the darkness night, when the union of the two halves is described evening is mentioned first. Just as the world begins in darkness, so does the day begin with evening. No longer regarded as chaotic, formless and void, this named and recognized darkness is given an ordered place within the world that God is making. What God has named, God will redeem. 'And God saw that it was good' (v. 10).

'And on the seventh day, God finished his work which he had done, and he rested on the seventh day . . . So God blessed the seventh day and hallowed it' (Gen. 2.2–3). The seventh day, like the preceding days, begins at sunset. God's rest begins with the night; the night is the source of refreshment and contemplation from which the restfulness of the morning and the afternoon must spring. When God blessed the day, both the evening and the morning were blessed.

We can see now how darkness has made progress. At first, it was regarded as a horrifying abyss, an amorphous nothingness, but then it was named and placed within the day. As such it was seen by God to be good. Goodness, however, was not enough. When we reach the seventh day, the darkness is not only good, it is sanctified by God's rest. It is declared to be holy. The darkness is blessed along with the morning and becomes the Sabbath of God. The God who brooded over the darkness, bringing it into the shape of separation and recognizing it, now completes this work by bringing the darkness and the light into a sacred unity.

I now realize that my first thought – that God is not on the side of the blind – was too hasty. God is the one who broods over blindness, calling it out of shapelessness and confusion, giving it a place of beauty and order in the fullness of creation. God blesses blindness and hallows it.

We read the Bible through the world in which we ourselves are embedded. When I was sighted, I read the Bible as a sighted person because I was embedded in the sighted world. It did not occur to me that I was sighted; I was just a normal person. Then I became blind. After the initial shock and the sense of alienation from my former life and my former world, once again I became a normal person. But the Bible seemed to have become abnormal. It came from a strange world – the world of sighted people, which was no longer mine.

In these chapters I will enter into conversation with the Bible from my point of view as a blind person. I describe these as conversations because I am conscious of the fact that what the Bible says to me has changed since I lost my sight. This is not only true of the places where there is specific reference to blindness, but of the text as a whole: when I realized that the Bible was written by sighted people, I felt alienated from it.

This book is the result of my gradually learning to begin a new conversation with the Bible – this time, as a blind person. It is mainly addressed to sighted people. Generally speaking, sighted people do not realize that they have a specific interpretation of the world. They just accept the world as a sighted world, because that is their experience. I hope that this book will do something to help sighted people realize the extent to which the Bible itself expresses their distinctive perspective.

Naturally, the book is also intended for blind readers who, like me, have passed beyond the light and are wondering where God is in the darkness.

People: First series

Isaac and Jacob: Blindness and deception

When Isaac was old and his eyes were dim so that he could not see, he called his elder son Esau and said to him, 'My son'; and he answered, 'here I am.' (Gen. 27.1)

Isaac has sent his elder son hunting, to prepare his favourite meal, in order to pass his fatherly blessing on to him before he dies. Isaac's wife Rebecca, overhearing the conversation, decides to take advantage of her husband's blindness in order to secure the blessing for Jacob, her favourite son. She dresses Jacob up in Esau's clothes, makes sure that his hands and the smooth part of his neck are covered with skin that is hairy like Esau's, and sends him in to his father with the kind of food that the old man loves.

When Jacob comes to his father he does not at first announce himself as Esau. He simply greets Isaac as 'my father'. Isaac in turn asks the question so often asked by blind people in this situation: 'Who are you?'

When you are greeting a blind person, you often have to act as though you were on the telephone. You announce yourself: 'Hello, this is . . .' Isaac knew, of course, that it was one of his sons – but he was not quite sure which one. It is, in essence, a question of expectations. It was rather too soon for Esau to be back, but he had no reason to suspect that the presence would turn out to be anyone else's. Quite often, when I am at home, I will hear an unidentified member of my family padding

around in the kitchen. I can usually tell who it is by the sound
of the footsteps, but I filter these sounds through my expectations of who it is most likely to be: if I am not expecting
someone to be in, I can make a mistake.

Then Jacob says, 'I am Esau your firstborn' (v. 19). The old
man is suspicious. No doubt this is not the first time Jacob
had played hide-and-seek with his blind father. Isaac questions
him and Jacob answers at a distance. It is not until Isaac
demands, 'Come near, that I may feel you, my son, to know
whether you are really my son Esau or not' (v. 21), that Jacob
approaches.

The results of the investigation are ambiguous. 'The voice
is Jacob's voice but the hands are the hands of Esau' (v. 22).
And so the old man appeals to the honesty and fair-mindedness
of his son. A big mistake: he already knows it is not Esau's
voice. 'Are you really my son Esau?' He hears the answer, 'I
am' (v. 24). He is given the food he especially likes and a bottle
of wine. All this time, the delicious smell from the hotpot must
have filled the tent. Isaac would be anxious lest the food should
get cold. Perhaps this is why he hurried the investigation.

Eating is often a problem when you are blind. Sometimes,
you get so sick of it: having to cut things, finding bones in
unexpected places, not being sure what you are eating half the
time. My own experience is that eating has become a bit of a
nuisance, while drinking has become quite important. Drinking
is so much easier. What you drink is in a cup, so it is easy to
find what you are after. There is no problem in getting it to
your mouth, especially after years of practice, and it is easy
enough to tell when you have finished. You never have the
embarrassment of sighted friends telling you where the last pea
on your plate is. You also become more sensitive, I think, to
the fragrance, taste and texture of the liquid.

Perhaps Isaac felt the same way. Like many blind people,
when the struggle to maintain the place of one's body in the
world with dignity and without accident has become tiring,
Isaac probably found it relaxing to have a drink or two. Some-

how your brain seems a little warmer, a little bit more at home inside your head, and you feel that the things that worry you don't matter so much.

In the meantime, however, Jacob takes no chances. He keeps his distance. After the meal, Isaac has to ask his son once again to come closer. The wine has mellowed him. 'Come near and kiss me, my son' (v. 26). With some trepidation, Jacob draws near and gives his father a kiss. It works out fine, because for the first time the old man notices Esau's clothes. They smell of the fresh air and the fields, the smell of Esau. So it is that Jacob receives the blessing.

As Jacob flees from Beersheba to Haran to escape his brother's anger, he probably thinks that he has left the world of blindness behind him. He has manipulated that world, so to speak, but there is more to the story. Jacob's uncle Laban has two daughters. The older sister is named Leah, and the younger Rachel. Leah's eyes are weak[1] but Rachel is graceful and beautiful (Gen. 29.17). Jacob thinks he is marrying Rachel but under the cover of the veil, the feasting and drinking and the night, Laban gives him Leah. Jacob protests to Laban that he has been deceived, but he does not get much sympathy from us. The one who had tricked a blind person is now tricked into marrying a weak-eyed woman. It is Leah, not Rachel, who first presents a child to her husband, because, she said, 'the Lord has looked on my affliction' (v. 32). It is the weak-eyed Leah who becomes the mother of Judah, the ancestor of David and of Jesus.

There are two more incidents in the life of Jacob that relate to blindness. The first event is emotional and symbolic; the second is his own old age and loss of sight. On his way home to meet his alienated brother Esau, Jacob sends his family and all his goods across the river Jabbok; he alone remains on the far side. And a stranger wrestles with him until the breaking of the day. When the stranger sees that he cannot prevail against Jacob, he strikes him on the hip socket and puts Jacob's hip out of joint. Then the stranger says,

'Let me go for the day is breaking.' But Jacob said, 'I will not let you go unless you bless me.' So he (the stranger) said to him, 'What is your name?' And he said, 'Jacob.' Then the man said, 'You shall no longer be called Jacob, but Israel, for you have striven with God and with humans and have prevailed.' Then Jacob asked him, 'Please tell me your name.' But he said, 'Why is it that you ask my name?' And there he blessed him. So Jacob called the name of the place Peniel, saying, 'For I have seen God face to face, and yet my life is preserved.' The sun rose upon him as he passed Peniel, limping because of his hip. (Gen. 32.26–31)

The fear of being attacked in the darkness by an unknown assailant must occur to many blind people. In times of loneliness and stress, this fear perhaps becomes more prominent. Once, when I was coming into the Education building at Birmingham University at night, I stretched out my hand to find the lift button and instead touched a man's jacket. I must have broken the Olympic record for an on-the-spot jump, because the security guard, who had been standing in the corner of the lift, said to me, 'Sorry, sir, I didn't mean to startle you.' 'But why didn't you greet me so that I would know you were there?' 'Sorry, sir.' I had apparently touched him before he could move away.

When Jacob is attacked by the strange figure, his experience must have been something like this. He does not know who is fighting with him or what he wants. He struggles blindly and anonymously and out of the struggle he emerges disabled but with a new identity. He has been touched by a dark angel and discovers that God is somehow present in his fight. I wonder if this experience gave Jacob some insight into the lives · of his blind father and his visually impaired wife.

In the closing years of his life Jacob, now also called Israel, experiences blindness for himself. 'Now the eyes of Israel were dim with age, and he could not see well' (Gen. 48.10). Israel's son Joseph, who had become the virtual ruler of Egypt, brings his own two sons to be blessed by their blind grandfather. The old man takes the little boys on his knees and kisses them. Then Joseph stands the children in front of Jacob and asks him to bless them. Manasseh is the elder, so Joseph places him by his grandfather's right hand. Ephraim, the younger, is placed by the old man's left hand, since the elder son should receive the more powerful blessing. To the surprise and consternation of the boys' father, the old man crosses his hands over, laying his right hand on the head of the younger son and his left hand upon Manasseh's. Joseph intervenes with a protest. He tries to lift his father's hand up from Ephraim's head, pointing out that it is Manasseh who is the elder of the two. 'But his father refused and said "I know, my son, I know; he also shall become a people, and he also shall be great. Nevertheless, his younger brother shall be greater than he ..."' (v. 19).

In those moments, did Jacob's mind go back to the time, so many years ago, when he, the younger son, had stood before his own blind father Isaac and deceitfully claimed his blessing? Does he wonder whether his son Joseph is deceiving him at this very moment, just as he had deceived Isaac? Would it not be poetic justice?

The narrator of the story has interests that go beyond poetic justice. The blind Isaac and the blind Jacob fulfil different roles. Isaac represents the weakness and vulnerability of blindness, the ways that a blind person can be exploited and manipulated. The blindness of Jacob shows us the strange insight that blind people are often thought to possess. Jacob knows which boy is which, or perhaps his hands know. The spirit of prophecy is upon him and he becomes not Jacob the deceiver but Israel the seer. Jacob the deceiver has passed through the dark night. He has wrestled with the angel of God and found a new identity. No such experience of terror and transformation is told of Isaac. Perhaps this is why the blindness of Isaac is unredeemed but the blindness of Jacob has become visionary.

Is blindness redeemable? Does the God of blindness have

ways of transforming blindness? 'My grace is sufficient for
you, for power is made perfect in weakness' (II Cor. 12.9).

Samson: Blindness and women

> So the Philistines seized him and gouged out his eyes. They
> brought him down to Gaza and bound him with bronze
> shackles; and he ground at the mill in the prison (Judg.
> 16.21).

If it is true that people differ in the balance of their senses, so
that some people are more tactile and others more aural, there
is no doubt that Samson is predisposed to sight. The very first
verse that describes his adult activities refers to what he sees.
Moreover, in this case it is not only the act of seeing but what
he sees that is to determine his fate over the next few years.
'Once Samson went down to Timnah, and at Timnah he saw
a Philistine woman' (Judg. 14.1).

The way he describes this to his parents is equally indicative
of a fully sight-centred man. '[He] told his father and mother,
"I saw a Philistine woman at Timnah; now get her for me as
my wife"' (Judg. 14.2). Samson does not say that he has met
her or that he has been introduced to her but only that he has
seen her. The sight is enough; he does not even mention her
name. When his parents rebuke him, Samson's reply is short
and to the point: 'Get her for me, because she pleases me' (v.
3). It is not until her next visit to Timnah that he talks to the
woman, and again we are told that 'she pleased Samson' (v.
7), but we are still not told her name.

The superficiality of the relationship based only on visual
beauty is shown in the dramatic story of the riddle that Samson
tells his guests during the wedding feast. When they cannot
guess the riddle, they threaten to destroy the woman's family
and property if she does not extract the answer from Samson.
Samson's response to her is characteristic of him. 'Look, I have
not told my father or my mother. Why should I tell you?'

(v. 16). Samson is really still just a huge muscle-bound adolescent, still closer to his parents and not yet capable of emotional intimacy. He takes it for granted that his relationship to his wife is not as confidential as the one he has with his parents. Samson's strength, physical passion and macho attitudes are evident in his bitter reply when he is taunted with the answer to his riddle: 'If you had not ploughed with my heifer you would not have found out my riddle' (v. 18). That just about sums it up: she is his heifer. In spite of her disloyalty to Samson, she does not escape the revenge of her own countrymen, for later on 'the Philistines came up, and burned her and her father' (Judg. 15.6).

Of course, the narrator makes out that all this has a political purpose. Samson is only seeking an occasion to attack the Philistines, who are the masters of Israel at this time. The way Samson carries out these threats – with such spontaneity, acting as an individual, taking advantage of his great speed and strength and his intimate knowledge of the countryside – are all typical of the sighted person. As a sighted man he fights with a young lion and tears it apart. It is almost as if he needs the madness of intense sexual frustration to work up the passionate fury that leads to his amazing exploits. It is after his wife has betrayed him that in anger he attacks the city of Ashkelon, killing thirty of its inhabitants and taking enough spoil to pay the forfeit demanded by the riddle contest (Judg. 14.19).

It's the same story when Samson is later denied access to his wife. His father-in-law (if the marriage really is recognized) tells him that she is no longer available. He has given her to Samson's best man and tries to palm Samson off with the offer of his younger daughter, who is even better-looking (Judg. 15.2). The idea that another man should decide which woman he is to have is quite sufficient to drive Samson into a fury, and in spite of the no-nonsense approach of the girl's father he goes out and burns the crops and olive orchards of the Philistines in an orgy of destruction. When the news reaches him that the Philistines have avenged themselves by burning both his wife and her father, his fury knows no bonds. 'He struck them down hip and thigh with great slaughter' (Judg. 15.8). He burns their crops; they burn his woman; he murders them. There is a simple, direct quality about Samson that is quite appealing.

Samson's next encounter with a woman is more or less the same, only minus the ceremony. 'Once Samson went to Gaza, where he saw a prostitute' (Judg. 16.1). There must be something terribly exciting about engaging in such behaviour right under the very noses, so to speak, of his enemies. Knowing Samson, the Philistines do not expect to see much of him before the morning, so they prepare to wait all night, until he comes out, in order to kill him. Samson surprises them by getting up early. Whether he is jubilant over his sexual success or frustrated that he has been interrupted halfway through the night, the story does not say, but in a characteristic blaze of power and energy he strips the city gate off its hinges and carries it up a nearby hill before his enemies can stop him.

Now we see a dramatic change. Of the next woman, we are not told either that he sees her or that she is fair, but only that he 'fell in love with a woman' (Judg. 16.4). Once again, she is a Philistine, so perhaps the motif of political provocation continues, but as always Samson's passions and his immense vitality get the better of his political judgement. He makes the mistake of loving a woman, and we know her name: Delilah.

There are two stories about the binding of Samson. On both occasions the binding is voluntary. The first time (Judg. 15.12–13), Samson agrees to be bound by his fellow citizens, as a pretext to allow him to get close enough to the enemy to destroy them. But when the Philistines surround him, 'the ropes that were on his arms became like flax that has caught fire, and his bonds melted off his hands' (v. 14). Grabbing the first thing he could lay his hands on, he kills a thousand of them.

Now is the first time that Samson is said to have prayed.

After all the killing, he is dying with thirst and he calls on the Lord, saying 'You have granted this great victory by the hand of your servant. Am I now to die of thirst?' (v. 18) He gets a big drink and goes on his way satisfied. Samson is quite a man – and only once more is he to offer a prayer.

It is remarkable that all of Samson's mocking answers to her questioning about the secret of his strength require Delilah to tie him up. Binding, fire and sex – these are the themes of the brilliant career of this sighted hero. The theme of outbursts of strength following sexual frustration is consistent.

> After this he fell in love with a woman in the valley of Sorek, whose name was Delilah. The lords of the Philistines came to her and said to her, 'Coax him, and find out what makes his strength so great, and how we may overpower him, so that we may bind him in order to subdue him; and we will each give you eleven hundred pieces of silver.' So Delilah said to Samson, 'Please tell me what makes your strength so great, and how you could be bound, so that one could subdue you.' (Judg. 16.4–6)

The first time Samson answers Delilah, he says, 'If they bind me . . .' Yet it is actually Delilah who does the binding (Judg. 16.8). He promises her that once he is bound with seven new bowstrings he will 'become weak, and be like anyone else' (v. 7). Not knowing that the Philistines are waiting in the next room, he must enjoy the thought of what he will do to her when he gets up, and this thought makes the binding all the more fun. She says to him, 'The Philistines are upon you, Samson!' The theme of fire enters into it again, for 'He snapped the bowstrings, as a strand of fibre snaps when it touches the fire' (v. 9).

> Then Delilah said to Samson, 'Until now you have mocked me and told me lies; tell me how you could be bound.' He said to her, 'If you weave the seven locks of my head with

web and make it tight with the pin, then I shall become weak, and be like anyone else.' (Judg. 16.13)

It is such a nice game that Samson tries it again. Once again, the Philistines will do the binding, as Samson says to Delilah, 'If they bind me with new ropes that have not been used, then I shall become weak, and be like anyone else', but as before it is Delilah who actually ties him up (vv. 11–12). Once again he gets the delightful anticipation of weakness turning into strength, of passivity turning into aggression, made all the more enjoyable by the fact that there are a few men to fight and chase away as well as a beautiful woman waiting for him when he gets back breathless and excited from the chase.

Samson no doubt thinks it is a pretty game, and Delilah certainly enters into the spirit of it. After all, the Philistines do not ask Delilah to bind him, but to entice him and find out wherein his great strength lies and how he can be overcome. The binding will presumably take place later. At first, Delilah is more or less faithful to this charge, and asks Samson 'Please tell me what makes your strength so great, and how you could be bound, so that one could subdue you' (v. 6). The second time she does not bother about the secret of his great strength and how he might be subdued, but comes straight to the point. 'Please tell me how you could be bound', and on the third time she does not even say please. 'Tell me how you could be bound' (vv. 10,13).

The third time the game is played, Samson tells more of the truth: he admits that the secret lies in his hair, which, when woven tightly, leaves him weak. With Samson the binding always has to be tight. In this act of the drama, a new motif enters: sleep. This is the first time we are told that Samson sleeps. In Gaza, when he has lain with the prostitute, we are not told that he slept, but only that he lay until midnight. Now at last, in the presence of the woman he loves, he closes his eyes.

After the third round, Delilah loses patience with the game

and Samson's lies. This time, she leaves binding out of it and
returns to her original request: 'you have not told me what
makes your strength so great' (v. 15). So at last he tells her
the secret of his religious identity. He is a Nazarite, under vows
never to touch strong drink and never to allow a razor to come
near his head (Judg. 13.5). In spite of all his violence, his
passions and his excesses, Samson has remained faithful to that
identity. It is the core of his being. Whatever else he does or
does not do, however many women he wants and gets, or loves
and plays with, however many men he kills, he remains in his
heart of hearts a Nazarite before God. This is the secret mission
laid upon his parents by the angel before his birth. It is because
of this that he can continue, in spite of everything, to be the
judge of Israel.

From this point, sight begins to pass from Samson to Delilah.
He tells her the truth: 'If my head were shaved, my strength
would leave me' (Judg. 16.17). Whereas until now Samson
has had the advantage of knowing the truth and has been
deceiving Delilah, now Delilah sees the truth and deceives
Samson.

Sleep is now a vital part of her plan. She lets him fall asleep
on her lap and calls a man to shave off the seven locks of his
head. She herself does not do the cutting; not only could she
not move without waking him, but the game is over. Typical
of Samson's passionate nature, however, is the fact that it is
not until she begins to torment him that he realizes that his
strength is gone (v. 9). Waking from his beautiful sleep, the
great riddle-master has the wrong answer. 'I will go out as at
other times, and shake myself free.'

Wake up, Samson, this time she has not tied you up! You
do not need to shake yourself free! You are free already, but
only for a moment longer. 'He did not know that the Lord
had left him' (v. 20). Does he not notice that his head has been
shaved? Does he not clap his hands to his scalp with a cry of
despair? No, he gets up to shake himself free as at other times.
But Samson, this is not like the other times. The Lord, who

was with you when you fought the lion, when you asked the riddle, when you paid for a woman, the Lord who was with you even when you killed a thousand men, has left you now. The taboo has been broken; the single fetish binding you to your religious childhood has been dissolved. After all, your strength did not lie in your huge shoulders and your massive arms, or in those bright eyes that have flashed with anger and desire so many times. Your strength lies in a promise made before your birth. Are you obliged, then, to keep that promise? It was not you who made it, but your parents. You were born into a promise, and with the broken promise your life itself is broken. 'So the Philistines seized him and gouged out his eyes. They brought him down to Gaza' (v. 21).

Samson knows Gaza, but to know a place as a sighted person is not the same as knowing it as a blind person. He had come before as a sighted man for pleasure and excitement; now he comes blind in agony and confusion. Does he brush past those great gates that once he had carried off so easily? Does he recognize the cobbled streets, the corner where the brothel is, as they hurry him on to the dungeons?

Not until the party arrives at the prison is there any reference to Samson being bound. The game is over. When they bind him finally, it is with shackles of bronze, and they set him to work grinding in the prison mill.

Samson works at the mill perhaps for months. At first the work seems hard, because he is now no stronger than any other man and has to cope with the shock of blindness and the physical pain of injury, to say nothing of the humiliation and despair that fill him. But the Philistines make a big mistake. They have forgotten to ask the prison barber to shave him anew every week. They have forgotten that lost identity can be restored. The promise of a religious childhood can be renewed, the memory of faithful parents can again stir in the heart. 'The hair of his head began to grow again after it had been shaved' (v. 22). The Philistines probably think that he is harmless now that he is blind, but the strength of Samson, although he was a vigorously sighted person, never lay in his eyes. The Philistines are sighted people and they misjudge a blind man. As is so often the case, they exaggerate the impact of his blindness.

We can only imagine what kind of sport the Philistines have with him in their big banqueting hall on the festival day. Do they dance around him, slapping him and striking him with rods, crying out 'Who struck you?' Do they pelt him with food and laugh as he tries to dodge? It must be something like this. If they brought out a lion to fight with him, as in the old days, the result might surprise them and they might just notice those long flowing locks.

When the sport is over, they make him stand between the two pillars upon which the roof rests. At this point, we learn something that is strangely moving: Samson has a young boy to hold his hand (16.26, RSV). He is not worth a couple of soldiers; a lad will do.[2] Does Samson think of the life of that boy, whose small hand is holding his? Does Samson somehow sense the presence of the pillars, or did he have an opportunity to make some contact with them during the sport? He knows those pillars are there. He senses that. That sixth sense, sometimes called facial vision, develops quite powerfully and fairly quickly in a state of total blindness. When Samson asks the boy to let him feel the pillars, it is not just to find out where they are. He needs both his hands and he no longer wants a boy to guide him.

On a previous occasion Samson prayed for his life when he was terribly thirsty. Once more he prays, not for his life this time but for his strength. In spite of his hair, he can never again take his massive strength for granted. Samson prays that God will remember him and that he will be revenged upon the Philistines for one of his eyes. Why not for both his eyes?[3] The idea is that even their violent deaths would not pay the price that Samson would demand for both his eyes. There are only about three thousand people on the roof. Samson's economic logic never falters. The crowd is worth one eye, no more.

Samson never gets revenge for his other eye, but dies with the three thousand in the ruin of falling masonry as the roof collapses. Does he whisper to the boy, at the last possible moment, 'Quick! Make a run for it'? The story does not say it, but I believe he does. Certainly there is no other trace of compassion in his life. As a blind man, he kills more than he has killed in all his sighted years. A determined and highly organized blind person, in the right place at the right time, can be most effective.

Eli: Blindness and the priesthood

> At that time Eli, whose sight had begun to grow dim so that he could not see, was lying down in his room. (I Sam. 3.2)

There did not seem to be anything wrong with Eli's sight some years earlier, since he had noticed Hannah's lips moving when she prayed silently in the temple for the birth of her child (I Sam. 1.12). It is possible, however, that his sight began to decline over the next two or three years, for when Hannah returns with the young child, he does not immediately recognize her. Hannah has to remind him and introduce herself by saying, 'I am the woman who was standing here in your presence, praying to the Lord' (I Sam. 1.26). Even then, Eli makes no sign of recognition or remembrance, although he certainly accepts the help of the child. Perhaps one reason why Eli is glad to have the boy is that his sight is getting poor and his own grown sons are completely unreliable. Eli's deteriorating sight is confirmed when we are told (2.22) that he hears of the extortion and sexual exploitation his sons are practising. Since they are doing all this quite openly, Eli sees it for himself, but it seems likely that blindness has undermined his authority; instead of strictly reprimanding them and forbidding them to do such things, he only asks in a mild sort of way, 'Why do you do such things?' Eli knows that people are talking about the behaviour of his sons (v. 24). On the other hand, when the unknown prophet of I Samuel 2.27 comes to warn Eli, he makes two references to Eli's sight. He is accused of looking with an envious eye at the sacrifices the people bring (v. 29), but in the days to come Eli will 'look with greedy eye on all the prosperity' (v. 32) around him.

Whatever the earlier history, and these are no more than hints, we are plainly told in I Sam. 3.2 that the sight of Eli has 'begun to grow dim, so that he could not see'. The near blindness of the old priest helps us to imagine the famous scene that follows. No doubt the child, or youth as he probably is by then, is accustomed to responding to the voice of Eli and has been trained to make himself known. He is used to running to him and saying 'It's me, Samuel!' When the Lord appears to Samuel, there is nothing visual about it. Perhaps by now Samuel has become accustomed to the idea that when the voice of a higher authority sounds, the proper response is to make it clear that you are indeed listening carefully and to announce who you are. This is the background against which Samuel says, 'Speak, for your servant is listening' (I Sam. 3.10). The auditory character of the experience is maintained in the message that God gives Samuel. 'See, I am about to do something in Israel that will make both ears of anyone who hears of it tingle' (I Sam. 3.11). Although Eli's reaction to the misbehaviour of his adult sons has all the features of the helpless plight of a blind old man who cannot see for himself that his sons are flirting with the women who stand in the very doorway of the house, and it is probably because his sons know he cannot check up on them that they venture to continue in their ways, the message of the Lord makes no concession to Eli's blindness. The fact is that he knew what his sons were doing (I Sam. 3.13) 'and he did not restrain them'.

The meeting between Eli and Samuel the following morning is typical. The old priest calls the name of the boy: 'Samuel my son?' and Samuel, in the usual way, replies 'Yes, it's me.' Now for the first time the old man shows a hint of passion, even of anger: 'What was it that he told you? Do not hide it from me. May God do so to you and more also, if you hide anything from me of all that he told you' (I Sam. 3.16–17). Eli has grown accustomed to not being told the full story and is probably afraid most of the time that he is not getting the whole truth. Here, however, he shows an anxiety, even an anger, that he does not display when he is trying to get the truth out of his grown sons. Then he merely entreated and begged. Now he commands. Is it because his sons are grown up and he is slightly afraid of them, but is not afraid of Samuel? Or is it that he does not recognize the voice of God speaking to him in anger through the injustice committed by his sons but, being a priest, is ready to receive the voice of God when it comes in a vision near the altar?

Another sign of Eli's lack of authority over his sons appears in I Sam. 4.4.

> So the people sent to Shiloh and brought from there the ark of the covenant of the Lord of hosts, who is enthroned on the cherubim. The two sons of Eli were there with the ark of the covenant of God.

There is no indication that either the people or Eli's sons seek Eli's permission to take the ark into the battle with the Philistines, nor, indeed, that Eli knows it has been taken. However, he soon hears, and now we find a sign that his sight, although very poor, is not entirely gone. During the battle, the old man is sitting on a bench by the roadside, 'watching, for his heart trembled for the ark of God' (4.13). However, the messenger who comes with the dreadful news does not report immediately to the man in charge of the sacred object, but spreads the news in the city first. The whole city gives a loud cry: 'When Eli heard the sound of the outcry he said "What is this uproar?"' (4.14).

Not until then does the messenger hurry to tell Eli the terrible news. Again, Eli's advanced age and blindness are emphasized: 'Now Eli was ninety-eight years old, and his eyes were set, so that he could not see' (4.14). It is possible that when the earlier comment is made about him sitting out by the roadside watching, this means merely that he is in a state of alertness: Eli likes to have people introduce themselves to him properly, because he cannot see them: the messenger has to say who he is and where he has come from. And Eli's death is typical of what might happen to an old, blind person: he loses his balance and falls backward from the bench (4.18).

When the old priest instructs the young boy Samuel to respond to the voice of God just as he would respond to his own voice, Eli is beginning to treat God as if God is also blind. When you come before the presence of God you have to announce yourself and tell him that you are listening. So a blind person starts to think of God as blind.

In his own old age, Samuel calls upon the people to bear witness that he has been faithful to his duties as a prophet, asking the people, 'from whose hand have I taken a bribe to blind my eyes with it?' (I Sam 12.3). The memory of the old priest's blindness, and how his indifference to justice had morally blinded him, stays with Samuel all his life.

Ahijah: Blindness and prophecy

> Now Ahijah could not see, for his eyes were dim because of his age. (I Kings 14.4)

After the death of Solomon, the Hebrew kingdom broke into a northern and a southern realm. Jeroboam, king of Israel's northern part, is not faithful to the tradition of worshipping only the God of Israel. When Jeroboam's young son Abijah becomes ill, it is decided that the Queen should go in disguise to the prophet Ahijah, taking gifts with her and presenting the boy as the sick child of an ordinary mother. Ahijah is well known to Jeroboam, since it was he who, in the days of Solomon, predicted that Jeroboam would become ruler of the northern kingdom (I Kings 11.29–39). However, Jeroboam must have known that his failure to keep faith with the God served by David and Solomon had brought him into disrepute with the old prophet. This is one of the reasons why he wants his wife to go in disguise with the child. Perhaps the seer will cure Abijah if he does not recognize him.

Ahijah, old and almost blind, lives at a shrine in Shiloh. With a kind of inspired intuitive knowledge, Ahijah knows that the Queen will be coming: and as soon as he hears her approaching, he cries out, 'Come in, wife of Jeroboam! Why do you pretend to be another?' (I Kings 14.6). Hearing her footsteps, he instantly recognizes the Queen.

It is not easy, in my own experience, to identify people by the sound of their footsteps. Of course, if you have some reason to expect them, then it is easier, and it also helps if there are a limited number of possibilities. In my own home, I can usually tell my wife Marilyn's footsteps on the wooden floor of the kitchen. My three sons are identifiable, most of the time, by their weight. My eighteen-year-old jumps and thumps down the stairs, taking them five or six at a time. My thirteen-year-old is almost as fast, but much lighter. Unless he is late for a TV programme, my ten-year-old usually walks more slowly, pausing here and there as he goes because something has caught his attention. As for my sixteen-year-old daughter Liz, it is often quite difficult to distinguish her steps from those of her mother. Carpeted floors do not help matters (I suppose the floor of Ahijah's shrine must have been tile or brick), nor do bare feet or soft-soled shoes. If there are visitors in the house, the sound patterns of footsteps become more complex and I am soon hopelessly confused.

Not so Ahijah. Ahijah, though blind, is a seer and cannot be deceived. He has insight. And intuition, the intuition so often attributed to blind people, can foil deception as well; although the child Samuel does not intend to deceive Eli, the intuition of the old priest tells him that it is the Lord God who is calling (I Sam. 3.2–9).

The Queen, at any rate, never stands a chance. 'I am charged

with heavy tidings for you' (I Kings 14.6) says Ahijah, and
tells her to deliver a terrible message from God to her husband
the King. 'You have not been like my servant David, who kept
my commandments and followed me with all his heart, doing
only that which was right in my sight' (I Kings 14.8). The
house of Jeroboam is to be destroyed and the entire nation of
Israel dispersed as well. And so Ahijah says to the mother,
'Therefore, set out, go to your house. When your feet enter
the city, the child shall die' (I Kings 14.12). Heartbreaking
through this news is, Ahijah goes on to explain that 'All Israel
shall mourn for him and bury him; for he alone of Jeroboam's
family shall come to the grave, because in him there is found
something pleasing to the Lord' (v. 13). In other words, all the
other members of the family will die violent deaths, but the
memory of the child will be honoured.

Throughout this story, images are recalled in a way characteristic of blindness. Jeroboam, reminded of how God tore the
kingdom away from David and gave it to him, is also reminded
of how he first came into contact with Ahijah, in the seer's
younger and sighted days. On an open road not far from Jerusalem, Ahijah tears the new robe he is wearing into twelve
pieces, gives ten to Jeroboam and tells him that ten of the
twelve tribes of Israel will follow him and break away from
the united monarchy (I Kings 11.29–39). As a blind person,
Ahijah would certainly remember the vivid tactile experience
of tearing the cloth, the sounds of ripping, the way the material
parted. He must often have meditated on that tactile memory
as he watched events unfold from his Shiloh shrine.

Through Ahijah, God says that Jeroboam has 'Thrust me
behind his back' (1 Kings 14.9). The metaphor is very close
to the experience of blind people. Even dropping something
always presents a problem of recovery, unless you are sitting
in a chair and can just feel around on the carpet. But if you
throw something violently behind your back, you might never
be able to find it again. That is what Jeroboam has done to
his faith in God, who in return will 'Consume the house of

Jeroboam, just as one burns up dung until it is all gone' (1 Kings 14.10). This is another image that is vivid without sight: the crackling of the flames, the acrid stench of the burning dung, the intense heat of the fire would all be part of the experience of the blind observer.

'The Lord will strike Israel, as a reed is shaken in the water; he will root up Israel out of this good land that he gave to their ancestors, and scatter them . . .' (v. 15). We can sit with Ahijah beside the reedy pool, hear the lapping of the water and the rustling as the breeze moves through the reeds. We can imagine him working his little vegetable patch at the back of the shrine, deftly pulling up the weeds and leaving the vegetables, having learnt to distinguish them by their feel.

There is a striking contrast between the pathetic figure of the blind Isaac, deceived by his crafty son, and the strong, courageous Ahijah, denouncing Jeroboam's kingdom and foretelling the death of the prince. Ahijah is blind, but he sees the state of Israel clearly enough. He sees the truth and speaks it fearlessly.

Zedekiah: The final blindness of the monarchy

> They slaughtered the sons of Zedekiah before his eyes, then put out the eyes of Zedekiah; they bound him in fetters and took him to Babylon. (II Kings 25.7)

When Jerusalem is destroyed by the Babylonians in approximately 597 BCE, Jehoiachin, king of Judah, surrenders himself to Nebuchadnezzar and is carried away into captivity in Babylon (II Kings 24.15). Jehoiachin's uncle is set up in Jerusalem as a puppet king and his name is changed from Mattaniah to Zedekiah. Nine years later, Zedekiah is foolish enough to rebel against Babylon and the city is again attacked. Seeing that the city is about to fall, Zedekiah and his retinue make their escape by night. They are pursued by the Babylonian soldiers, captured and brought back to Nebuchadnezzar for punishment.

The sons of King Zedekiah are killed and he is blinded.

Zedekiah is about thirty-three years of age by this time, so his sons must be quite young, probably still children. The peculiar cruelty in the act lies in the boys' execution just before their father is blinded; the last memory of Zedekiah's sighted life, which he carries with him until the last, is the sight of his dying children.

We do not hear of Zedekiah again. Presumably he spent the rest of his life as a blind slave in a foreign land, like Samson, except that in his case there was no restoration, no growing of the hair. And so the line of kings that began with David comes to an end. David had beautiful eyes (I Sam. 16.12) but the eyes of Zedekiah are put out. The royal line that began with beautiful eyes finishes in blindness.

Tobit: Blindness and family life

Tobit is the only book in the Bible to have blindness as its central theme. It is also the only book named after a blind person. Moreover, it is the first biblical account of the healing of blindness, being about three hundred years older than the stories from the Gospels about Jesus' miraculous healing of blind people.

Tobit is a slighted person when the story begins and when it ends. Perhaps it would be more correct to say that the central motif in the book is the losing and regaining of sight, rather than blindness as such. Tobit is a sort of blind Job. He is renowned for his righteousness, suffers a strange and almost inexplicable affliction and is healed, but whereas the book of Job is presented (after the opening and closing sequences) as a philosophical and theological poem of great beauty and power, the story of Tobit is told in simple, graphic detail almost as a folk-tale.

The story is set amongst the exiled people of Israel, who have been carried away captive into Nineveh, the capital of the Assyrian empire. The story opens, however, in Israel itself, where we read about Tobit's faithfulness to God, how careful he is to observe all the requirements of divine law. He is brought up an orphan, but learns his religious duties from his grandmother, Deborah. He always visits Jerusalem with the produce of his land and contributes to the city's maintenance. He marries Anna and their son Tobias is their only child. After the destruction of the northern kingdom and the transportation of the survivors to Nineveh, he continues his religious observance. From time to time persecution breaks out against the Jews, and Tobit makes a special point of making sure that the bodies of any who are killed are decently buried. When this becomes known to the authorities, his property is confiscated and he escapes with only his life, returning to Nineveh, where his wife waits with a beautiful meal prepared to celebrate his homecoming.

True to his generous nature, Tobit refuses to eat unless poor and hungry people from the city share his meal, and he sends his son, Tobias, to invite them. But the boy returns from this errand with the news that the body of a strangled Jew is lying in the market-place. Tobit immediately runs out and hides the body in a safe place, intending to return at night to bury it. After returning home to eat his meal in sorrow, he goes back out, digs a grave and buries the body. Disaster follows. Unwilling to return to his home until he has washed and purified himself, he sleeps out of doors that night; as he sleeps, sparrow droppings fall into his eyes and he is blinded.

Apparently what really happened was that Tobit developed cataracts, which medical folklore attributed to sparrow droppings. It is interesting to note that this is the only case in the Bible where blindness is attributed, however naively, to natural circumstances. Elsewhere, people's sight deteriorates with increased age (Isaac, Jacob, Eli) or people lose their sight through acts of violence (Samson, Zedekiah) or divine intervention (Paul, Elymas). None of these options are available here. Tobit could not be too old, for it is necessary that his son Tobias should still be a young man and unmarried. To have his eyes put out by violence would be contrary to the general impression of the respect and high standing which the family and acquaintances of Tobit enjoy in the government, and no motive suggests either demonic or angelic intervention. The demon is preoccupied elsewhere, as we shall see, and there is no reason in the story why God should punish Tobit, whose life is exemplary.

Although there is no hint of divine retribution upon Tobit, he himself is inclined to attribute his blindness to God. He prays that God will not punish him for his sins, or for anything he has done unintentionally. He wonders if he is being punished for the sins of his predecessors (3.3). He wonders whether his blindness is part of the general punishment to fall upon the people of Israel: 'Your many judgements are true in exacting penalty from me for my sins' (3.5).

This is often the reaction of religious people when they suffer adversity. Being sensitive in conscience and accustomed to walking closely in the presence of God, they quickly conclude that the hand of God is present in the calamity. On the whole, religious people tend not to give sufficient weight to the element of randomness in life. Looking for secret purposes and mysterious causes, we are liable to underestimate the spontaneity and freedom of the world. Faith in God does not mean that we must poke and pry at every event to find some strange purpose behind it. Sometimes things just happen.

Tobit, at any rate, is a sensible character. His first response to his blindness is not to search his conscience for a reason for divine punishment, but to seek medical assistance (2.10). The doctors are not able to help, and the first problem Tobit faces is typical of the dilemma into which blindness throws people. He is deprived of his means of support.

This is often the case with people who lose their sight. Some years ago, I was invited to speak to a group of men, all of whom had lost their sight in adult life. When I had finished telling my story, there was a moment of silence. Then one of the men said, 'Well, I have heard what you have to say, and

I much admire the way you have been able to cope, but there is one thing you must not forget. You did not lose your job when you lost your sight, but every other man in this room has become unemployed because of blindness.' I realized sharply that I was one of the lucky ones. If I had been a taxi driver, or a brain surgeon, or a security officer, this would have happened to me as well. Being a university teacher, as long as I had my voice and my brain, I could still function.

Tobit is not so lucky. For a while, his nephew Ahikar, highly placed in the administration of the kingdom (1.22), is able to support the family. But when this benefactor is posted to another district, Tobit's wife, Anna, is forced to find a job. On one occasion, as a little bonus, her employers give her a kid goat. For some reason, Anna does not immediately tell Tobit about the gift, or perhaps he hears it bleating before she has a chance to tell him; in any case, he leaps to the conclusion that Anna has stolen it. How desperate the family has become, and how overwhelmed Tobit must be by his poverty and dependence! It is so easy for a blind person to lose confidence in the daily affairs of life, when he or she feels excluded from the decisions and has a sense of uselessness.

Tobit refuses to believe Anna, though she defends herself robustly, crying out, 'Where are your charities and your righteous deeds? You seem to know everything!' (12.14, RSV). If I had been Tobit, and Anna had said that to me, I would have heard, 'What has happened to your character since you lost your sight? You were once so full of confidence in people but now you don't even trust your own wife. Once you yourself did good deeds for everyone; now you are so bitter that you cannot believe that someone did a good deed for me.'

It is natural for Anna to feel such anguish. She might well believe that her husband's punctilious attention to duty has cost them their independence and their happiness. Once so active in the community, her husband is now reduced to a complaining, suspicious shadow of his former self.

This misunderstanding between husband and wife brings the

pain of loss to the surface as nothing has before. This is the moment when Tobit breaks down and weeps, acknowledging that his blindness is God's punishment, pleading for his life to end. 'It is better for me to die than to live, because I have had to listen to undeserved insults, and great is the sorrow within me' (3.6). In his bitterness and grief, Tobit is only able to state half of the truth. He has indeed heard a false reproach from his wife, but cannot acknowledge that he made the first false approach when he accused his wife of being a liar and a thief.

The story then moves to the distant city of Ecbatana, where we find a young woman whose prayer is similar to Tobit's. Sarah is desired by the evil demon Asmodeus, who jealously slays every man she marries on their wedding night. So far seven young men have perished in this way, and not unnaturally Sarah has become rather discouraged (as have the young men of the district). Her maids are taunting her and she feels her life not worth living. Like Tobit, she prays for God to take away her life. 'Command that I be released from the earth and not listen to such reproaches any more' (3.13).

Having established the parallel between the two people, one afflicted with blindness and the other under a terrible erotic curse, who are both praying for release from life, the plot now turns toward resolution. 'The prayers of both of them were heard in the glorious presence of God' (3.16). Tobit and Sarah finish their prayers at the very same moment, and God sends the great angel Raphael to answer them. He comes to remove 'the white films from [Tobit's] eyes' (3.17) and to see that Tobias marries Sarah and the evil demon is suitably punished.

The first movement in the drama of restoration takes place when Tobit remembers that he has left a large sum of money in the care of a trusted friend in a distant city. Although convinced that he is about to die, he thinks it only reasonable to make sure that his son Tobias and his widow Anna have the benefit of the funds. It is strange how blindness, sorrow and loss sometimes seem to stimulate the memory: in a moment of despair, one remembers something important, something that might change everything. Before the blind man's eyes can be restored, his memory has to be restored.

When Tobias, accompanied by his dog and the stranger who has been hired as a guide (who is really Raphael), set out on their journey, Anna breaks out in weeping, sure that she will never see her son again. With sad and poignant words, the blind father comforts his sighted wife. 'Do not worry; our child will leave in good health and return to us in good health. Your eyes will see him' (5:21). Yes, Tobit is thinking, your eyes will indeed see him, but mine will never see him again. Even if I am still alive, I will never have the joy of seeing his smiling face as he returns to greet us.

Camping on the banks of the Tigris river, Tobias catches a huge fish, and the angel tells him to keep the heart, liver and gall; the smoke from the burning heart and liver, says the angel, will drive away any demon, whilst the gall will heal cataracts. Ecbatana, where Sarah lives, is on their route and, with the angel's help, Asmodeus is driven away and the young lovers unite in marriage.

Meanwhile, back in Nineveh, Tobit and Anna are increasingly concerned about the return of their son and new daughter-in-law. Once again, the issue between them is one of deception. On the matter of the kid, Tobit has accused Anna of deceiving him; now the situation is reversed. Tobit is confident that the travellers will return, but Anna replies, 'Stop trying to deceive me! My child has perished' (10.7). It is so easy for trust to break down between blind and sighted people. Are the sighted people exchanging glances between each other even as you speak? Is there some expression in their eyes which is hidden from you? Has a letter arrived which they have not told you about? From the point of view of the sighted person, there is a question about the thoughts of the blind person. I once heard one of my sighted friends say to her husband during a discussion, 'Open your eyes! I don't know what you are thinking about!' That made me think that sighted people depend upon visual contact for mutual understanding. This is one of the reasons why blind people, from the point of view of sighted people, become enigmatic.

These issues are brought out vividly in the reunion scene. 'Meanwhile Anna sat looking intently down the road by which her son would come' (11.5). Tobit is forced back into himself. He has only his prayers and his thoughts. He has to depend upon Anna for the information for which he longs as much as she does. In spite of her irritation with him, Anna is sensitive to this and must realize the dilemma between them. When she catches sight of Tobias in the distance, 'She said to his father, "Look, your son is coming"' (11.6). It would be more natural, perhaps, to say, 'Tobias is coming' or 'Our son is coming', but when she says, 'Your son is coming', she shows awareness of the distance that blindness has created between the returning young man and his father. 'Then Anna ran up to her son and threw her arms around him, saying, 'Now that I have seen you, my child, I am ready to die' (11.9). The author of the story seems to highlight the independence which Anna has as a sighted person. 'I have seen you,' she cries out, almost as if she is trying to compensate for the fact that Tobit will never, as she then believes, be able to say those words to his son. Tobit also gets up to run out but stumbles and so his son runs to him. This is a common experience for a blind person. One is always left until last, left waiting on the porch while everyone else runs off down the drive, each thinking that someone else is bringing you.

Tobias applies the gall of the fish to his father's eyes and 'rubbed off the white films . . . Then Tobit saw his son and threw his arms around him, and he wept' (11.13–14). Now that his sight is restored, independence is also his. His first use of his newfound mobility is to go to the gate of the city where his daughter-in-law Sarah is waiting for him. 'When the people of Nineveh saw him coming, walking along in full vigour and with no one leading him, they were amazed' (11.16). Blindness is a very visible condition. There can be little doubt as you watch someone walk along the road, especially if they are

hurrying or even running, that they can see. I am reminded of
the story in Matthew's Gospel of how Jesus said to the two
blind men whose sight had been restored, 'See that no one
knows of this' (Matt. 9:30). It was impossible for them to
prevent people from knowing about it, because as soon as their
friends, neighbours and relatives saw them coming, it was clear
that they were no longer blind. When Tobit greets Sarah he
makes no mention of his former blindness. His words of greeting are, 'Come in, my daughter, and welcome. Blessed be your
God who has brought you to us, my daughter. Blessed be your
father and your mother' (11:7). Why should he mention it?
Sarah has never seen him as a blind person and never would.
Tobit must often have imagined that reunion, how he would
embrace his son, who would introduce Sarah – but how
would he greet Sarah? What would she make of him? Was she
familiar with blind people? How easy would it be for them to
get to know each other? All these doubts and questions are
now resolved. He has gone out on his own two feet and
welcomed his daughter-in-law.

The song of praise from Tobit with which the story ends
makes it clear that Tobit, in spite of the literal character of his
blindness, is a symbol of the exiled nation. The idea that the
people are metaphorically blind in the sense that they did not
understand or obey the covenant with God was already well
established in the prophets before the exile, so a story in which
a blinded representative of Israel receives sight is a symbolic
expression of hope. The fact that the blindness is caused acci-
dentally, and yet at the same time is somehow within the general providence of God, is nicely expressed in the story of
the sparrow droppings, and expresses Israel's moral sense that
though they brought exile and the destruction of Jerusalem
upon themselves, it is nevertheless part of the movements of
history over which they have no control.

It is surprising that the commentaries on Tobit seldom refer
to the centrality of blindness as the major theme of the story.[4]
This, however, is re-emphasized in the final chapter of the

book, where we are told that Tobit was sixty-two years old[5] when he became blind and he remained blind for a period of eight years.[6] His blindness is thus a relatively brief interval in his life, especially since he lives to be 112 years old (14.2).

Before Tobit dies, he speaks of the glorious rebuilding of Jerusalem and the worldwide conversion of the Gentiles to faith in the living God. The exile will be but a painful interlude in the continuing dealings of God with Israel, just as blindness has been a painful but relatively brief chapter in his own life. Tobit uses the metaphors of light and darkness once again in his farewell speech (13.11). He speaks of being brought from darkness into light and of falling back into darkness (RSV). No doubt the memory of his own descent into darkness remains with Tobit all his days, as a solemn symbol of the destruction of his sighted life.

2

People: Second series

The Gospel of Matthew: Two anonymous blind people

As Jesus went on from there, two blind men followed him,
crying loudly, 'Have mercy on us, Son of David!' When he
entered the house, the blind men came to him; and Jesus
said to them, 'Do you believe that I am able to do this?'
They said to him, 'Yes, Lord'. Then he touched their eyes
and said, 'According to your faith let it be it done to you.'
And their eyes were opened. Then Jesus sternly ordered
them, 'See that no one knows of this.' But they went away
and spread the news about him throughout that district.
(Matt 9.27–31)

Two blind men follow him. No doubt they help each other
along, as blind people do. The more adventurous one walks
slightly in front, holding whatever is the first-century equivalent of a white cane, while the more timid one, or the one
who is less familiar with the place, walks slightly behind him,
holding on to his elbow or his coat.

I used to have a fine research student who was not only blind,
but a woman and a priest of the Church of England. She had a
little bit of sight and a dog, while I had no sight and no dog,
but a long white cane. When we travelled together, we were the
world's most formidable couple. The crowds melted before us
and crowded footpaths were cleared as quickly as if there had
been a bomb warning. Striding across a concourse, we would
cut a swathe, like a mower going through a hayfield.

In a restaurant, she had the advantage, for the dog could find us a free table and a couple of unoccupied seats. On a train, I had the advantage, since with the long cane I could go to the buffet and buy drinks, whereas she would wait for the steward and ask him or her to get drinks. A dog handler must walk beside the dog, not way behind or in front, and in the aisle of a train there is no room for a person and a dog to walk side-by-side.

Another blind student of mine was from one of the Caribbean Islands. She was totally blind and a nun, and carried a white cane like mine. Sometimes we walked around the campus. I would take the lead when it was part of the campus I knew, and when we were on some of her routes, she would lead. When surprised students asked us if we needed any help, she would reply with a laugh, 'No, thanks my dear. We'se folks is just a-goin' for a liddle walk!' Yes, it is quite fun when you are with another blind person, just walking along.

Our two blind men are not just walking along; they are following Jesus. They keep shouting out, as blind people do. If you have ever been to a meeting of blind people, you will know what I mean. The door opens and instead of slipping quietly into a seat, the newcomer calls out, 'Hi everyone, is this such-and-such a meeting? I'm Harry.' Everyone in the room calls out, 'Hello Harry, I'm Judith, Thomas, Hilda' and so on. Every time this happens, the chair has to start reading the minutes all over again.

It is rather easier when you are following a crowd, as these two men are. People make a noise and you just track after the noise. You may lag a little bit behind, if the crowd is moving fast, but you still hear them and you still keep shouting. The noise dies down and the sound of footsteps fades away. You realize they have all gone inside somewhere. You are pretty close behind and you soon detect the sound from inside the house. Finding the doorway is not difficult and now, at least, it is possible to catch up. That is why the blind men can come to Jesus when he enters the house.

The next part of this story is perplexing for many blind people. 'Do you believe that I am able to do this?'

In 1952 I was in the Sixth Form at Melbourne Boys High School preparing for university matriculation examinations. I was seventeen years old and had just suffered a retinal detachment in the left eye. This was the first problem that had arisen since my cataract operations three or four years earlier. Although I kept a careful record of the progress of the detachment, drawing diagrams week by week in a diary in order to monitor the slow progress of the dark disc across my field of vision, I had had no previous experience of detachments and had no idea what it was. Unfortunately, the eye specialist who was consulted was unable to detect the detachment or explain the loss of sight. Vision in my right eye was quite good, although since the cataract operation, which had the effect of dissolving the lenses, I had worn very thick spectacles. I suppose they did not know then that this type of cataract operation is frequently followed by detachment. At last, the detachment was virtually complete and my left eye could only make out bright shapes and movements, seen, as it were, from the bottom of the sea through a shifting, wobbly, jelly-like green and yellow ocean. Two years later the right eye would also become detached, but this time I had expert ophthalmological attention in a leading Melbourne hospital.

Back in 1952, however, neither my parents nor I knew what to do. At that time an American evangelist was visiting Melbourne. His healing ministry was well publicized, and the newspapers carried exciting advertisements. The deaf were receiving their hearing, the lame were walking, cancer was being cured and, most exciting of all to us, the blind were receiving their sight.

My father and mother were Methodists of a conservative evangelical outlook, and so was I. We had no particular links with the pentecostal movement but we had heard of faith healing and knew something of the ministry of the healing evangelists. Above all, we were steeped in the stories of Jesus and, although we had never discussed the healing miracles in connection with my own problems, I suppose they were at the back of our minds. Whether it was my mother's suggestion or mine I cannot remember, but one evening we decided to attend one of the meetings.

When we entered the large hall, it was already crowded, and before long the choir came on stage and the singing began. After some preliminaries, the evangelist himself came on stage and, after a long exhortation, called upon people who were seeking healing to walk down the aisle, come up on to the stage and meet him. Stewards were available to help people whose mobility problems were so great that they could not get up the steps to the stage. All this time the singing continued while the evangelist called upon the sick and the disabled to have faith in the power of God. The tension was mounting and all around us people were raising their hands in prayer, calling upon Jesus to have mercy on them, and a few people were beginning to move down the aisles. We watched amazed as someone coming up on to the stage with crutches walked off the stage without them. The building rocked with shouts of praise.

'What do you think then? Shall I have a go?' I whispered to my mother. She nodded her agreement and down the aisle I went. On the stage I was met by a steward who asked me what my problem was. I told him that I was almost blind in one eye. There were others in front of me, but finally it was my turn.

The steward presented me and told the evangelist what was wrong. Facing me inside a barrage of microphones, the healer asked me, 'You are blind in one eye?' 'Well,' I replied, 'pretty nearly blind.' Placing his hands upon my head he cried out, cursing the blind spirit which had possessed me and calling upon Jesus Christ to drive out the blind spirit and restore my sight. He withdrew his hands and told me to cover my good eye with one hand. I did this, then he pointed to a clock on the wall of the auditorium and asked me if I could see it. The face of the clock, which must have been a good two feet across, was brightly illuminated and, following his pointed finger, I could see the glow of light on the wall. 'Yes,' I stammered, 'but I could see that anyway.' The moment the first word 'Yes' was out of my mouth, the evangelist grabbed the microphone: 'Hallelujah! He can see!' The whole auditorium erupted with shouts of praise and two powerful ushers grabbed me, one by each arm, and marched me firmly from the stage. The tightness of their grip and the immediacy of the response left me in no doubt that their action was fully intended to curtail my protest. Stumbling down the aisle, I found my mother weeping. Tapping her on the shoulder I said, 'It's just the same, Mum. Come on, let's go home.' Although I have been approached by faith healers many times since then, this was the only occasion when I actually sought faith healing. The incident left a deep impression upon me. I knew now that the crowd were being deceived. I wondered whether the person before me with the crutches had been planted by the organization. Was the evangelist party to this deception, or was he a victim of his own wonderful oratory? Was he self-deceived as well as deceiving, and was he being exploited by those big stewards with the strong grip? I had no way of knowing.

There seem to be several contrasts between the work of the modern evangelist and that of Jesus. In the first place, Jesus did not invite the two blind men to come to the house; they followed him, shouting, and entered of their own accord. Many of the modern healing evangelists, however, invite people to attend their meetings and then encourage them to come forward to the stage. Moreover, they make no end of a fuss about their healings. They seem to want as much sensational visibility and public reputation as possible. Jesus, however, sternly charged the once-blind men, 'See that no one knows of this.'

Whatever the motivation of Jesus in placing the men under this constraint, or whatever the motive of the Gospel author in attributing such commands to Jesus, it certainly reads in rather a strange way. How could people help knowing about the miracle? Jesus did not command the blind men not to tell anybody, which would in itself be difficult enough, but that no one was to know. Two blind men suddenly appear amongst their friends and relatives seeing. When this happens, it is not necessary for the previously blind people to point to their eyes and say 'Look! Now I can see!' It is obvious to everyone who sees them that they can see. Anyway, we are told that the once-blind men went away and 'spread his fame through all that district'. Whether they did this by disobeying Jesus and actually telling people or whether it was the inevitable result of their appearance, we can only imagine. The unreal nature of the demand which Jesus is said to have placed upon the two men does suggest that this idea is an intrusion into the original story, possibly initiated by Matthew himself, as part of his attempt to explain why, at a later date, hardly anybody believed in Jesus.

The Gospel of Mark: The blind man from Bethsaida

In the Gospel of Mark we are told about two people whose sight is restored by Jesus. The first incident is described in Mark 8.22–26: 'Some people brought a blind man to him and begged him to touch him.' This blind person is more passive than the one described in 10.46–52, Bartimaeus. Of course, since Bartimaeus is a professional beggar, he is naturally sitting beside the road looking for handouts. This is how he comes to hear the crowd and realizes that Jesus is passing. The blind person in chapter 8 is simply brought by his friends. The friends beg Jesus to heal him; the blind man himself makes no comment. Perhaps he had become used to other people speaking on his behalf. Every time he lines up at the village well for a drink of water, it is the person with him who is asked the question. When Marilyn and I go to the bank together so that I can transact some business over the counter, she actually has to walk away in order to compel the clerk to deal with me. Otherwise the questions are always addressed to her. It is not only wives and husbands but also dogs who have this effect upon the public. One of my blind friends told me that the greatest blow to her self-esteem she ever suffered was when she got her guide dog. People spoke to the dog and ignored her. Sometimes people would bend down to the dog's ear and whisper travel directions to the dog. The dog not only acted as her eyes but even as her intelligence. She liked her supervisions with me because I ignored the dog altogether. After all, the dog was quiet and I did not realize it was with her.

'He took the blind man by the hand and led him out of the village' (Mark 8.23). This is surely one of the most beautiful and moving incidents regarding blindness in the entire Bible. True enough, Jesus did not use the normal way of guiding a blind person, which is to extend one's elbow so that the blind person can put a finger under the elbow or a hand over the arm. This gives a blind person the greatest possible sense of independence, since he or she is walking along and not being held, drawn or pulled. It is a test of the maturity, common sense and experience of a sighted person to allow a blind person to touch the elbow. Some sighted people want to grab your arm, lock it tightly into place with a vice-like grip and propel you forward. Others complain that they cannot feel the touch of your finger on their elbow through their clothes. I always say, 'Well, don't let that worry you. I can feel you and that's what matters.' The best and most experienced sighted guides give the blind person credit for having enough gumption to hang on. Anyway, this is a mere detail. The main point is that Jesus acts as a guide to this blind person. To hold by the hand is a gesture, not only of support, but of intimacy. What must it be like to hold the hand of Jesus? Would I venture to ask him to let go and explain to him that it is better to lead with the elbow?

There are all sorts of suggestions about why Jesus led the man out of the village. It was probably because Jesus wanted privacy, and in this respect he is very different from the modern faith healers who love crowds and publicity.

and when he had put saliva on his eyes and laid his hands
on him, he asked him, 'Can you see anything?' And the man
looked up and said, 'I can see people, but they look like
trees, walking.' (Mark 8.23–24)

Here we have the famous healing in two stages. The fact that
Jesus asks the man whether or not he could see anything
suggests that he himself is not quite sure whether the healing
has been effective. When the man, now only partially-sighted,
says that he can see people like trees walking, 'Jesus again
laid his hands upon his eyes ... and he looked intently
and his sight was restored, and he saw everything clearly'
(Mark 8.25).

In spite of the saliva magic which seems to lie behind this
story,[7] we should probably not interpret it in the first place as
a nature miracle, where the folk remedy has to be applied
twice. Rather, it is a parable or symbol of the blindness of the
disciples.[8] Several times during the gospel Jesus rebukes his
disciples for their failure to understand him; so the period of
partial vision should probably be regarded as the experience
of the disciples before the resurrection of Jesus, and the restoration of full sight would then refer to the insight which the
church had into the person and meaning of Jesus after the
resurrection, the ascension and the day of Pentecost.

The problem is why the great apostles who founded the
churches did not themselves understand the meaning of Jesus
during his own ministry. Why did Jesus generally not find that
people had faith in him? The answer that this symbolic healing
seems to suggest is that faith did not come from association
with the early Jesus, but only from incorporation into the
Trinitarian life of God, when the Church, enlightened by the
Holy Spirit, understood the truth about Jesus. It is not a question of being literally blind but a question of understanding or
not understanding Jesus. Paul says, 'Even though we once knew
Christ from a human point of view, we know him no longer
in that way' (II Cor. 5.16); in other words, our faith is not

provoked by the ministry of Jesus, even by the wonderful healings, but only by life in the Spirit.

Nevertheless, whatever its symbolic meaning, we can still
imagine the incident at its face value. It must have been
wonderful to be led by the hand of Jesus.

Bartimaeus: Blindness and poverty

> They came to Jericho. As he and his disciples and a large
> crowd were leaving Jericho, Bartimaeus son of Timaeus, a
> blind beggar, was sitting by the roadside. When he heard
> that it was Jesus of Nazareth, he began to shout out and say,
> 'Jesus, Son of David, have mercy on me!' (Mark 10.46–47)

The passage in Mark 10 is more dramatic. Being supported by
one's family or begging must have been common ways of life
for blind people in the ancient world, as they are today in
certain countries. Bartimaeus must have become an expert
interpreter of crowd noises. He would be familiar with the
short, light steps of children, the heavier tread of men, the
hesitant paces of old people and the sound of a woman's footsteps, sometimes clarified by a snatch of conversation or a
whiff of perfume which would settle the doubt. Bartimaeus
hears the steady march of a detachment of Roman soldiers
before anyone else, and he is the first to become aware of
something unusual happening.

There is excitement in the air. A large crowd is coming.
Quick enquiries soon reveal the answer: it is Jesus of Nazareth.
The name of Jesus had probably gone like wildfire around the
communities of sick and disabled people in the area. Bartimaeus knows that this is his opportunity. Indeed, such a chance
might never come again.

His sight is gone but there is nothing wrong with his voice.
There is no point in getting up and pushing through the crowd.
He would only get pushed aside and lose his sense of direction.
In the confusion, Jesus might pass by. So he stays right where

he is, sitting beside the road, and begins to shout at the top of his voice. 'Jesus, Son of David, have mercy on me!'

> Many sternly ordered him to be quiet, but he cried out even more loudly, 'Son of David, have mercy on me!' (Mark 10.48)

There is something slightly disturbing about shouting. To the orderly mind, it suggests a possible rebellion, an excess of emotion which is inappropriate. It is said that on one occasion a rather formal, middle-class congregation was electrified by a sudden shout of 'Praise the Lord!' which came from a member of the congregation. A stern-faced elder dressed in a black suit walked steadily down the aisle, tapped the offender on the shoulder and said, 'This is a Presbyterian church. We'll have no praising the Lord here.'

It is like this when Bartimaeus shouts out. People try to hush him. All around him people are telling him to shut up, but he can tell that the bulk of the crowd is now almost directly opposite and he increases his volume. Over the noise of the crowd, Jesus hears his cry. The story then continues with one of the most expressive and moving sentences in the Gospels. The record simply says, 'Jesus stood still' (v. 49). What sensitivity, what quality of attentiveness is in that sentence. Just as when the woman with the haemorrhage touched the fringe of his garment and the disciples were surprised that, hemmed in by the crowd and amidst the pushing and shoving, he had detected the touch which was an entreaty (Mark 5.25–34). So now, above the babble and confusion, he hears the voice with its hint of desperation, 'have mercy on me.'

Jesus says, 'Call him here.' Now the attitude of the crowd changes. 'You're okay mate. He's heard you.' 'Come on, get up! He's calling for you.' Bartimaeus springs up, throws off his cloak, and many willing hands thrust him forward. The crowd parts and there is silence. Then Bartimaeus hears a voice, which he knows must be the voice of Jesus, asking him a most surprising question. 'What do you want me to do for you?' (Mark 10.51).

Jesus does not actively seek out blind people and offer them healing. He is not a healing evangelist of the modern type, who advertises healing as a regular part of his ministry. Of course, there were stories of strange and wonderful happenings, and no doubt the visually handicapped community, in so far as it was a community, had heard these stories. Otherwise Bartimaeus would not respond so remarkably to the news that Jesus is coming. However, there is little or no indication that Jesus sent messengers ahead, calling visually handicapped people to gather together in the market square, or perhaps the synagogue, to await his arrival. The truth is that he would have passed by if Bartimaeus had not shouted out so loudly.

Even now, face to face with him, Jesus makes no assumptions about what the man wants. This shows a remarkable and gracious acceptance. Jesus does not take it for granted that the man wants his sight restored. He offers the man the dignity and independence of declaring his request. Nowadays, the blind person would have said, 'Get me some computer training and a job with a firm which has a decent equal opportunities policy', but this story is not set in the modern world. Bartimaeus says, 'Master, let me receive my sight.' And Jesus says to him, 'Go your way; your faith has made you well' (v. 52, RSV).

The words of Jesus are given fresh meaning when we think of them from the point of view of Bartimaeus. 'Go your way.' In his life as a blind person he had not been able to go his own way, but had depended upon others and had to follow in the ways that they chose. Now at last he can go his own way. 'Immediately he regained his sight, and followed him on the way' (v. 52).

The way that Bartimaeus chooses is the way of discipleship. This reminds us that the story of his healing is intended to be a symbol or parable of conversion.[9] In becoming a disciple of Jesus, you are delivered from the ignorance and helplessness of your former life and given direction and purpose in living. This symbol expresses the sighted person's point of view. To be delivered from the restrictions of blindness into the freedom of a sighted person's life is one of the most desirable transformations that a sighted person could imagine. Naturally, blind people get caught up in this point of view.

This puts blind people into a difficult position. What are we to say in reply to the question of Jesus, 'What do you want me to do for you?'

Sometimes when sighted people are urging me to take advantage of the visit of a famous healing evangelist and I hesitate, they say to me, 'But wouldn't you like to have your sight restored?'

What should I say? Would I not like to see the smiling faces of my family? Would I not like once again to have the freedom and spontaneity which mobility gives to sighted people? Would I not like to go shopping by myself and travel alone for fun to strange places? Would it not be as if the whole world were given back to me again?

The question is unfair. It is like the question, 'When did you stop beating your wife?', or perhaps more like the question which pacifists are sometimes asked, 'Would you defend your wife if she were attacked by a would-be rapist?'

There is a sense in which the advantages of sight are so obvious that no one would prefer to be blind. In the same way, the advantages of having two legs are so obvious that no one would prefer to have one leg or none. The advantages of being loved are so obvious that no normal person would prefer to be unloved. Who would not prefer freedom to bondage, health to sickness, wealth to poverty?

A man who had been blind for many years wrote to me saying that even after all these years he still occasionally had dreams in which he had perfect sight. His question was, 'Do we ever lose the fantasy of perfect vision?' I think the answer to that question is no. If you have had sight once and can remember vividly the colour and movement, the excitement and spontaneity of that life, you never lose a certain fantasy of restoration. It is on that fantasy that the would-be faith healer exercises his manipulatory power. Here is a letter which I received late in 1997.

Dear Mr Hull,

There is fortunately, a type of healing that is known as divine healing. It is done by Christians laying their hands on needy and afflicted persons. There is a man by the name of Peter Scothern who has been mightily used of God in divine healing. He conducts divine healing services in various areas of Britain. He goes to various areas, if invited to do so, to lay his hands on needy and afflicted persons.

A person, writing on your behalf, could invite Scothern to come to Birmingham University to lay his hands on you. A person, writing on your behalf, to invite the Rev. Scothern to come to Birmingham to conduct a divine healing service in the University or church or hall. The address of Scothern is [address supplied]. If you intend having a divine healing service in Birmingham, you could inform all the needy and inflicted in Birmingham of the coming service. The needy persons of Birmingham will be as follows; blind, semi-blind (especially those blind with injured eyes and those blind because they have not got eyeballs), deaf and semi-deaf, dumb, those in continuous pain, diseased [*sic*] (especially those with diseases what are thought to be 'incurable' in the opinion of most persons), allergic (especially those with the worst allergies), and those who have lost the ability to taste or to smell, those with bronchial troubles, and those with mental troubles, and those who are physically abnormal, and many others with other things wrong with them. The parents of these needy persons should also be informed of the coming service. DIVINE HEALING CAN IRADIC-ATE BLINDNESS [*sic*]. DIVINE HEALING CAN ACHIEVE THINGS THAT DOCTORS AND SUR-GEONS CANNOT ACHIEVE.

I am sending a leaflet that will inform the reader of the miraculous restoration of sight to [name].

The Rev. Scothern sends leaflets about divine healing and about the gospel through the post. He also sends through the post, MIRACLE PRAYER CLOTHS. A prayer cloth can be laid on the inflicted [*sic*] or abnormal part of the human anatomy, combined at the same time with prayer in the name of CHRIST. A prayer cloth could be laid on the eyelids of the BLIND, combined at the same time with prayer in the name of JESUS. THE KNOWLEDGE OF DIVINE HEALING SHOULD BE SPREAD AS SOON AS POSSIBLE TO THE NEEDY AND INFLICTED. ALSO THE EXISTENCE OF SCO-THERN AND HIS ADDRESS AND DIVINE HEAL-ING SERVICES AND MIRACLE PRAYER CLOTHS, SHOULD BE MADE KNOWN AS SOON AS POSSIBLE TO THE NEEDY AND ABNOR-MAL, AND TO THEIR PARENTS.

Yours sincerely
J. P. Morris

Here is my reply:

Dear Mr Morris

You wrote to me recently about the healing ministry of Mr Scothern. There are a number of misunderstandings in your letter which I thought you would like me to correct.

In the first place, you describe me as being needy and afflicted. Of course, in a sense I am needy, as are all human beings. However, I am much less needy than many. God has blessed me in many ways. I have a wonderful wife and five beautiful children. Because I have been able to do useful work for my employer, the University of Birmingham, I have a secure job and am able to maintain myself and my family at a standard of living which is higher than many in our country. As for being afflicted, it is true that I am blind.

However, I do not interpret my blindness as an affliction, but as a strange, dark and mysterious gift from God. Indeed, in many ways it is a gift that I would rather not have been given and one that I would not wish my friends or children to have. Nevertheless, it is a kind of gift. I have learnt that since I have passed beyond light and darkness, the image of God rests upon my blindness. No sighted person can say that he or she is beyond light and darkness and yet we are told in Psalm 139, v. 12 that God is beyond light and darkness. So in that respect it seems to me that it is blind people who are in the image of God rather than sighted people. Because of their dependence upon outward appearance and their confidence of being superior, it is often sighted people who are needy and many of them could do with a good dose of blindness, like Tobit or St Paul in the Bible, to bring them a kind of humility and insight which has not come to them through sight.

I am a Christian like yourself. My Christian life has been deepened since I lost my sight. This loss has helped me to think through many of my values in living, and in a way I have learnt a greater degree of intimacy with God.

Your letter distressed me because it showed so little sensitivity to the actual condition of blind people, and no awareness at all of the emotions and beliefs of Christian blind people. You assume that everybody wants to be like you, a sighted person, and you do not recognize that people are called into various states of life, some of which they would perhaps rather not have had, but they grow in faith and realize that whether sighted or blind they are in the hands of a merciful God.

Thank you for your letter and I hope that my response will help you to consider again the Christian values behind your own letter.

Yours sincerely

The Gospel of John: Blindness from birth

> As he walked along, he saw a man blind from birth. His disciples asked him, 'Rabbi, who sinned, this man or his parents, that he was born blind?' (John 9.1–4)

Although people sometimes claim that the reply of Jesus, 'Neither this man nor his parents sinned; he was born blind so that God's work might be revealed in him', indicates that Jesus did not believe in the connection between blindness and sin, there are other parts of the record which suggests that Jesus did accept a link between sin and disability. For example, when Jesus finds the lame man who had been healed at the Pool of Bethesda in the temple, he says to him, 'See, you have been made well! Do not sin anymore, so that nothing worse happens to you' (John 5.14). Around the pool there 'lay many invalids – blind, lame and paralysed' (John 5.3). Presumably Jesus shared the common belief that they were all there because of some sin.

Another example is the paralysed man described in Mark 2.3–12, who had been lowered through the roof to Jesus. Jesus says to him, 'Your sins are forgiven.' It is only later, when he is challenged about these words, that he commands the lame man to get up and walk. The suggestion that there is a connection between the sin and the paralysis is inescapable.

In the case of the blind man in John 9, however, Jesus explicitly denies any connection between blindness and sin. Rather, the man has been born blind in order to provide a sort of photo opportunity for Jesus. The idea is that God is glorified when Jesus restores the man's sight, and for this he has been blind all his life.

Although blindness is symbolic of sin and unbelief in the three earlier Gospels, it is in the Fourth Gospel that this connection reaches its climax. John's Gospel was the first book in Braille that I read after I had become blind in my adult life. As I read it, rather laboriously, I was delighted to have access once again to so many familiar and greatly loved passages. However, the symbolism made me feel uneasy and I soon came to realize that this book was not written for people like me, but for sighted people. No other book of the Bible is so dominated by the contrast between light and darkness, and blindness is the symbol of darkness. This reaches its climax in chapter 9, the central miracle of the Gospel, the man born blind. The perspective of the sighted person is illustrated in the words that follow immediately. 'We must work the works of him who sent me while it is day; night is coming when no one can work' (John 9.4). I do not know whether blind people found work during the time of Jesus; did they know how to weave baskets and mats? Were there blind potters and even blind carpenters? At any rate, it is certain that the coming of night does not stop blind people from working. As far as this particular blind man was concerned, he certainly had no work, because people said, 'Is not this the man who used to sit and beg?' (v. 8).

The parallel between blindness and unbelief, sight and faith, is emphasized in verse 39:

'I came into this world for judgement so that those who do not see may see, and those who do see may become blind.' Some of the Pharisees near him heard this and said to him, 'Surely we are not blind, are we?' Jesus said to them, 'If you were blind, you would not have sin. But now that you say, "We see", your sin remains.' (John 9.39–41)

This reaffirms the thought in the opening verses, that there is no connection, at least in this case, between blindness and sin. Sin lies in the self-deception of those who believe that they have insight but do not.

I was speaking at the Religious Education Association Annual Conference in Indianapolis in 1992 and happened to be standing at the entrance to one of the restaurants that opened off the hotel courtyard. Two or three people passed me, entering the restaurant. A man stopped and said to me, 'Are you blind?' 'Yes', I replied, wondering what would happen next. 'And are you with this religious conference?' was the next question. When I told him that I was, he let out a loud laugh and pronounced triumphantly, 'Well, you better not be, or you won't be able to believe your own stuff!' Having floored me with this masterpiece of witty logic, he and his party went on down into the restaurant, chuckling.

I was nine years old when my parents took me to see a skin specialist in Melbourne. Two doctors examined the flexes of my elbows, which were covered with eczema. One said to the other, 'How old is he?' 'Nine.' 'Oh no, he's not nine. More like nineteen!' The last speaker then said to me, 'What does your father do? Isn't he a minister?' 'Yes.' 'And what are you going to be?' 'I'm going to be a minister too.' 'Well, you'd better make sure your skin clears up or you won't be able to believe your own preaching.' I came away feeling rather pleased at what I took to be a compliment about my maturity, and rather puzzled and perhaps alarmed at the thought that perhaps I might not be able to be a very good minister.

In Birmingham, a taxi driver said, 'Do you mind if I ask you a personal question?' 'Go ahead.' 'What did you do that God made you blind?' 'Well, nothing more than what most people do, who don't become blind.' 'Well, maybe you were going to do something bad.' 'You mean God would have known about this in advance and made me blind in order to stop me doing it?' 'Yes.' 'Well, I don't particularly remember planning a bank robbery or anything like that.' Here the conversation ended. I quote these examples, taken over a span of more than fifty years and from three continents, to show that belief in the connection between sin and sickness or disability is still widespread. Of course, it is perfectly true that some kinds of sinning can ruin your health, but to attribute sin to every sick person is to add a burden of social disapproval and guilt to a person who is already suffering. I suppose I should have had the quickness to say to the man outside the restaurant, 'And

what great act of holiness did you do, in order to make you
so healthy?'

Paul: Blindness denied

Now as he was going along and approaching Damascus,
suddenly a light from heaven flashed around him. He fell
to the ground and heard a voice saying to him, 'Saul, Saul,
why do you persecute me?' He asked, 'Who are you, Lord?'
The reply came, 'I am Jesus, whom you are persecuting. But
get up and enter the city, and you will be told what you
are to do.' The men who were travelling with him stood
speechless because they heard the voice but saw no one.
Saul got up from the ground, and though his eyes were
open, he could see nothing; so they led him by the hand and
brought him into Damascus. For three days he was without
sight, and neither ate nor drank.

Now there was a disciple in Damascus named Ananias.
The Lord said to him in a vision, 'Ananias.' He answered,
'Here I am, Lord.' The Lord said to him, 'Get up and go to
the street called Straight, and at the house of Judas look for
a man of Tarsus named Saul. At this moment he is praying,
and he has seen in a vision a man named Ananias come in
and lay his hands on him so that he might regain his sight.'
But Ananias answered, 'Lord, I have heard from many about
this man, how much evil he has done to your saints in
Jerusalem; and here he has authority from the chief priests
to bind all who invoke your name.' But the Lord said to
him, 'Go, for he is an instrument whom I have chosen to
bring my name before Gentiles and kings and before the
people of Israel; I myself will show him how much he must
suffer for the sake of my name.' So Ananias went and entered
the house. He laid his hands on Saul and said, 'Brother Saul,
the Lord Jesus, who appeared to you on your way here, has
sent me so that you may regain your sight and be filled with
the Holy Spirit.' And immediately something like scales fell

from his eyes, and his sight was restored. Then he got up and was baptized, and after taking some food, he regained his strength. (Acts 9.3–19)

In the speech which he made in Hebrew to the great crowd assembled in the temple some years later (Acts 22), Paul refers to this experience:

> While I was on my way and approaching Damascus, about noon a great light from heaven suddenly shone about me. I fell to the ground and heard a voice saying to me, 'Saul, Saul, why are you persecuting me?' I answered, 'Who are you, Lord?' Then he said to me, 'I am Jesus of Nazareth whom you are persecuting.' Now those who were there with me saw the light but did not hear the voice of the one who was speaking to me. I asked, 'What am I to do, Lord?' The Lord said to me, 'Get up and go to Damascus; there you will be told everything that has been assigned to you to do.' Since I could not see because of the brightness of that light, those who were with me took my hand and led me to Damascus.
>
> 'A certain Ananias, who was a devout man according to the law and well spoken of by all the Jews living there, came to me; and standing beside me, he said, 'Brother Saul, regain your sight!' In that very hour I regained my sight and saw him.' (Acts 22.6–13)

The details of the experience are slightly different. In the account which Luke, the author of the Acts of the Apostles, gives in chapter 9, it is not at all clear that Paul himself saw the light. His experience seems to have been mainly, if not entirely, aural. Perhaps he fell from his horse to the ground, stunned by the light, but verse 7 tells us that his companions heard the voice but saw no one. It does not even say that they saw the light or were dazzled by it. They seemed to be unaffected by the brightness but they did hear the voice. For them as well, therefore, it was primarily aural.

However, when Paul describes the experience himself in chapter 22, still reported of course by Luke, the aural aspect is minimized and the visual is emphasized. 'A great light from heaven suddenly shone about me' (22.6), and Paul's companions 'saw the light but did not hear the voice of the one who was speaking to me' (v. 9). Moreover, this account does not exactly say that Paul became blind. 'I could not see because of the brightness of that light' (v. 11). In other words, Paul was dazzled. The character of the blindness is also minimized in the second account (vv. 12–13). Certainly, Ananias says to Paul, 'Regain your sight', but nothing is said about scales falling from Paul's eyes. Indeed, the expression 'I regained my sight and saw him' is difficult to derive from the Greek. *Anablepo* can mean either to see again or to look up; *eis auton* means 'at him'. The translation 'I received my sight at him' sounds very strange, but 'I looked up at him' does not really suggest the restoration of sight, as the context seems to require. Aware of the difficulty, most translators try to have it both ways, hence the usual English version, 'I received my sight *and* looked up at him' or 'I received my sight and saw him'.[10]

The idea is that the restoration of Paul's sight was less a miracle than a blessing in which the dazzling effect disappeared, and in that sense he received his sight and was able to look up at Ananias. Moreover, if this really was a miraculous restoration of a blind person, it is the only case in the New Testament where a miracle is carried out by the miracle worker alone, without reference to the name of Jesus. The omission of the scales falling from the eyes helps to convey the idea that this has been more a temporary lapse of sight rather than an explicit blindness which had to be miraculously restored. In order to create that impression, it was necessary to enhance the light phenomenon (in order to account for the dazzle) and consequently to downplay the aural aspects.

The Damascus road experience is described for a third time in Acts 26, where Paul is shown defending himself in the presence of King Agrippa:

'At midday along the road, your Excellency, I saw a light from heaven, brighter than the sun, shining around me and my companions. When we had all fallen to the ground, I heard a voice saying to me in the Hebrew language, "Saul, Saul, why are you persecuting me? It hurts you to kick against the goads." I asked, "Who are you, Lord?" The Lord answered, "I am Jesus whom you are persecuting. But get up and stand on your feet; for I have appeared to you for this purpose, to appoint you to serve and testify to the things in which you have seen me and to those in which I will appear to you. I will rescue you from your people and from the Gentiles – to whom I am sending you to open their eyes so that they may turn from darkness to light and from the power of Satan to God, so that they may receive forgiveness of sins and a place among those who are sanctified by faith in me."

'After that, King Agrippa, I was not disobedient to the heavenly vision, but declared first to those in Damascus, then in Jerusalem and throughout the countryside of Judea, and also to the Gentiles, that they should repent and turn to God and do deeds consistent with repentance.' (Acts 26.13–20)

Now we notice something truly remarkable. The blindness of Paul has completely disappeared. Moreover, the visual aspects of the experience are furthered emphasized. The light is now 'brighter than the sun' and is seen by both Paul and his companions, all of whom fall to the ground. In the mandate from the Lord which follows, emphasis is placed upon the things which Paul has seen and will continue to see (v. 16) and, most striking of all, the blindness is transferred from Paul to the recipients of his message. It is they who are in blindness, not he, and their eyes are to be opened. They are to turn from darkness to light in response to the Christian message (v. 18). Here we see the familiar arrangement of meanings: blindness is associated with darkness, the power of Satan, experiencing the weight of unforgiven sin and being excluded from the company of those who are sanctified through Christ (v. 18). Paul, or at least his interpreter Luke, has increasingly forgotten his blindness, or found it convenient or tactful to omit it when defending himself in public. The mystery of why Paul (then Saul) should have been afflicted with blindness, even temporary blindness, at the very moment when he was summoned to obedience by Jesus Christ must have been almost as great a mystery as the crucifixion of the one appointed by God to be God's Messiah. To be crucified was to be under a curse (Gal. 3.13), but by a paradoxical inversion the curse fell upon those who had crucified him. In a similar way, to be blind was to be under a curse, but a similar paradoxical inversion had brought Paul into the light of a glorious heavenly vision and thrust the objects of his mission into blindness.

This all presupposes that blindness is indeed a curse from God, but we must ask whether what Paul experienced was punitive blindness. We may contrast the blindness of Paul with the blindness of Elymas Bar-Jesus (Acts 13.6–11). The similarities lie in the suddenness and the fact that the blindness was only temporary. Moreover, both men were actively engaged in hostility to the Christian message when they were abruptly halted by the onset of blindness. These similarities were close enough to be a source of embarrassment.

However, in other respects it is doubtful if Paul's blindness was thought of as a punishment. In the case of Elymas, there are words of rebuke and cursing which call down the blindness upon the magician, but in the case of Paul there is no such curse. Indeed, the words of Jesus to Paul are supportive and encouraging. He is told to get up and go into Damascus. There is no hint at all that he will not be able to go into Damascus until someone leads him. The comment 'I am Jesus whom you are persecuting' is not really a rebuke, but an identification of the speaker, together with perhaps a touch of ironic reproach. Jesus reveals himself as being present in the church which Paul is persecuting. Paul himself offers no protest or hesitation.

The blindness of Paul can be compared to the dumbness of Zacharias when the angel Gabriel told him that Elizabeth was to bear a son. He replied, 'How will I know that this is so? For I am an old man, and my wife is getting on in years' (Luke 1.18). The angel announces that he will be dumb until the birth of the child, 'Because you did not believe my words' (v. 20), but after all, what the old man said is no worse than what Mary herself says to the angel, 'How can this be, since I am a virgin?' (v. 34). Mary is indeed a highly favoured one, since the angel takes her comment in good spirit and gives her an answer, but at the same time they are both highly favoured. Both have received messages from God through the angel, in each case message of great joy, and in the case of Zacharias an answer to a heartfelt prayer. So although there is a punitive element in Zacharias' dumbness, it is very slight. The archangel does not curse Zacharias or dramatically smite him. Of the three of them, Zacharias, Mary and Paul, Paul is the most receptive, since he does not demur in the least. Why then should he be smitten with blindness?

We must also compare the blindness of Paul with that of Tobit, which was caused, so the story says, by sparrow droppings falling into his eyes. There is not a hint of reproof or punishment about this incident, which appears to be purely natural. Another similarity is the way that, at the time of the healing, scales seem to fall from their eyes. This feature only occurs the first time that the story is told in Acts, and would hardly be consistent with the idea that Paul was merely dazzled. This is probably why the detail about the scales falling from Paul's eyes does not occur when, according to Luke, Paul himself is telling the story. It seems fairly clear that Tobit and Paul are both examples of non-punitive blindness.

The blindness of Tobit, however, is symbolic of the unbelief of Israel which led to the exile. That is how Tobit himself interprets it. The restoration of his sight is a symbol of the restoration of Israel. Could we say that the blindness of Paul was symbolic of the blindness of the Jews in not believing

Christ, and the restoration of his sight was symbolic of the restoration of Israel to faith in Christ? This seems improbable because, on the whole, Jews did not respond to the message of Paul or the other Christian evangelists. As Paul remarked rather ruefully, 'that same veil is still there' (II Cor. 3.14). Moreover, we have the additional difficulty that if the blindness of Paul was intended to be symbolic of the unbelief of Israel, surely he would have been struck down with blindness when he set out on the Damascus road, breathing threats and curses against the Christians, and not immediately after the vision in which Christ called him as a special instrument of God's favour.

The blindness of Paul thus remains a difficulty. Paul himself and his historian Luke were evidently aware of this and underplayed it, especially in controversial situations when they were explaining the mission to hostile audiences. Because of its difficulty, and the fact that it had to be explained away, it is likely that Paul's blindness was indeed grounded in fact. In view of the negative attitude of the Bible towards blindness, it seems most unlikely that a feature like this would have been added to the story of St Paul's apostle calling, thus creating all the problems we have discussed. The fact that it remains resistant to complete disappearance indicates the kernel of historical truth within it.

At the moment when he was confronted by Jesus of Nazareth, Paul realized that his former life had been based upon a false premise. Using the negative metaphorical language common to the Bible and every sighted culture, he was overwhelmed by the realization of his 'blindness'. Just as Zacharias was dumb until John was born to him, so Paul remained blind until he was born anew into faith in Jesus Christ through the Holy Spirit (Acts 9.18). The strange nature of this delayed birth is suggested by Paul's description of it in I Cor. 15.8. 'Last of all, as to one untimely born, he appeared also to me. For I am the least of the apostles, unfit to be called an apostle, because I persecuted the church of God.' As he was greeted by

Ananias, the first representative of Jesus Christ whom he had not sought to persecute, and thus brought into Christian fellowship, the scales fell from his eyes and he was baptized. Thus he came to hope that those who, in the chaos of an unborn life, had like him been plunged into profound misunderstanding would also be brought to life and knowledge through faith in Christ. They also, as they were born to Christ, would pass as it were from darkness into light. Paul's blindness was thus not punitive. It was not inflicted upon him by God or by Jesus. It was a kind of revelation, a judgement formed about his own life. It was not so much Paul's eyes that were blind as his whole life that had been misdirected.

Paul was, after all, not far from the truth when he said that he had been dazzled by that exceedingly great light. In the brightness of the knowledge of Christ, all his previous knowledge seemed but darkness. The scales were added later by Luke, who has a tendency to describe things in physical terms, possibly remembering how the blindness of Tobit came to an end.

Elymas: Blindness as punishment

Although the Bible contains plenty of references to blindness as a punishment, there are only two unambiguous cases of it actually taking place. The first is recorded in Genesis 19, where Lot the nephew of Abraham has invited two angelic visitors to spend the night in his house.

But before they lay down, the men of the city, the men of Sodom, both young and old, all the people to the last man, surrounded the house; and they called to Lot, 'Where are the men who came to you tonight? Bring them out to us, so that we may know them' [One must remember the sexual connotation of the verb 'to know' in Hebrew.] Lot went out of the door to the men, shut the door after him, and said, 'I beg you, my brothers, do not act so wickedly. Look, I

have two daughters who have not known a man; let me
bring them out to you, and do to them as you please; only
do nothing to these men, for they have come under the
shelter of my roof.' But they replied, 'Stand back!' And they
said, 'This fellow came here as an alien, and he would play
the judge! Now we will deal worse with you than with
them.' Then they pressed hard against the man Lot, and
came near the door to break it down. But the men inside
[the angelic visitors] reached out their hands and brought
Lot into the house with them, and shut the door. And they
struck with blindness the men who were at the door of the
house, both small and great, so that they were unable to
find the door. (Gen. 19.4–11)

It was a terrible thing that Lot was about to do to his daughters.
Were they to be thrown out into the street and raped all night
so that his two visitors could be protected? Had not his daughters also come under the shelter of his roof? However, there
is another dreadful aspect of this story. It sets up a connection
between sexual violence and blindness, and particularly
between blindness and homosexuality. In the case of Samson,
there is an association between sexuality and blindness, but at
least Samson's loss of sight was not directly inflicted upon him
by God. In the case of Sodom, the blindness was directly
inflicted by the angels, and although, no doubt, it seemed at
the time an effective way of protecting the household, in the
long run it has set up associations with blindness which are
anything but helpful. On the one hand, the blind are supposed
to be pure and innocent, because it is impossible for them to
look lustfully upon another person, but on the other hand,
there is often this hint of some earlier misdemeanour.

In the case of the magician Elymas Bar-Jesus, there was no
suggestion of sexual misconduct. Rather, it is a case of blindness as a punishment for deliberately seeking to obstruct the
Christian message.

When they had gone through the whole island as far as Paphos, they met a certain magician, a Jewish false prophet, named Bar-Jesus. He was with the proconsul, Sergius Paulus, an intelligent man, who summoned Barnabas and Saul and wanted to hear the word of God. But the magician Elymas (for that is the translation of his name) opposed them and tried to turn the proconsul away from the faith. But Saul, also known as Paul, filled with the Holy Spirit, looked intently at him and said, 'You son of the devil, you enemy of all righteousness, full of all deceit and villainy, will you not stop making crooked the straight paths of the Lord? And now listen – the hand of the Lord is against you, and you will be blind for a while, unable to see the sun.' Immediately mist and darkness came over him, and he went about groping for someone to lead him by the hand. When the proconsul saw what had happened, he believed, for he was astonished at the teaching about the Lord. (Acts 13.6–13)

The similarities between the blindness of Elymas and that of Paul himself are quite striking. Paul had also been opposing and obstructing the gospel, and in both cases the blindness was temporary. Perhaps Paul remembered his own experience of blindness and had a moment of pity for Elymas in telling him that he would only be blind 'for a while'. Paul is led by the hand into Damascus; Elymas goes around seeking someone to lead him by the hand, and we are not told if anyone helped him or not. The blindness is the work of the hand of God and is preceded by a terrible curse. On the other hand, if it had not been for the blindness of Elymas, Sergius Paulus, the proconsul, might not have accepted the Christian message, so the blindness of one led to the insight of the other.

Although the stories of the men of Sodom and Elymas the magician are unique, we must read them against a background of a general expectation of blindness as a punishment.

[God] frustrates the devices of the crafty, so that their hands achieve no success. He takes the wise in their own craftiness, and the schemes of the wily are brought to a quick end. They meet with darkness in the daytime, and grope at noonday as in the night. (Job 5.12–14)

Sometimes blindness is inflicted not upon the evildoers but upon their children. 'Those who denounce friends for reward – the eyes of their children will fail' (Job 17.5). The plight of the wicked person is described as follows: 'darkness so that you cannot see; a flood of water covers you' (Job 22.11). The psalmist complains of how God has afflicted him: 'My heart throbs, my strength fails me; as for the light of my eyes – it also has gone from me' (Ps. 38.10). When the psalmist pronounces curses upon his enemies, he says, 'Let their eyes be darkened so that they cannot see' (Ps. 69.23). Considering their miserable situation after the destruction of Jerusalem and the way that they have been chastened for their sins, the prophet Isaiah says of his people,

> Therefore justice is far from us,
>   and righteousness does not reach us;
> we wait for light, and lo! There is darkness;
>   and for brightness, but we walk in gloom.
> We grope like the blind along a wall,
>   groping like those who have no eyes;
> we stumble at noon as in the twilight,
>   among the vigorous as though we were dead . . .
> For our transgressions before you are many.
>
> (Isa. 59.9–10, 12)

When the prophet Zephaniah is describing the coming Day of the Lord, we read, 'I will bring such distress upon people that they shall walk like the blind; because they have sinned against the Lord, their blood shall be poured out like dust' (Zeph. 1.17), while the passage in Zech. 11.17 could apply to the false prophet Elymas Bar-Jesus himself. 'Oh, my worthless shepherd, who deserts the flock! May the sword strike his arm and his right eye! Let his arm be completely withered, his right eye utterly blinded!'

Not only was the sin of Israel rewarded with blindness but, as in the story about the Sodomites, blindness was a favourite threat or curse against the enemies of Israel. Even the horses in the armies of the enemies shall be blinded. 'On that day [the day when the Lord will rescue Judah], says the Lord, I will strike every horse with panic, and its rider with madness. But on the house of Judah I will keep a watchful eye, when I strike every horse of the peoples with blindness' (Zech. 12.4); and on the day when the Lord restores Jerusalem, 'This shall be the plague with which the Lord will strike all the peoples that wage war against Jerusalem: their flesh shall rot while they are still on their feet; their eyes shall rot in their sockets, and their tongues shall rot in their mouths' (Zech. 14.12). When wicked people are making plots against the righteous, their plans will come to nothing: 'Thus they reasoned, but they were led astray, for their wickedness blinded them' (Wis. 2.21). Later in his book, the author of Wisdom reminds his readers of the blindness of the Sodomites. Speaking of the wicked of his own day he says, 'They were stricken also with loss of sight – just as were those at the door of the righteous man – when, surrounded by yawning darkness, all of them tried to find the way through their own doors' (Wisd. 19.17). In the story as told in Genesis, the blindness prevented the aggressors from finding the door of Lot's house, but here in this later version the men of Sodom are depicted as being unable to return to their own homes.

Blindness was not only thought of as a punishment and the result of a curse, but was also used as a term of ridicule and abuse. When the prophet Isaiah ironically invites the enemies of Jerusalem to come and capture it (56.10), he points out that they will have an easy time: 'Israel's sentinels are blind, they are all without knowledge; they are all silent dogs that cannot bark; dreaming, lying down, living to slumber'. This reminds us of the passage in II Samuel (5.6–8) where the inhabitants of Jerusalem in an earlier age taunt David's men by saying that even blind people could defend the city against them.

The psychological effects of all this on those who were without sight must have been horrific. The estimate which blind people form of themselves is a mirror image of the view of blindness held in the surrounding society. If you have always consciously or unconsciously thought of blind people as pathetic and incompetent, when you become blind yourself you adopt an image of yourself as pathetic and incompetent. One of the most common reasons for disabled people losing their jobs is the low self-image which is the result of the initial impact of their disability, a low image with which their employer readily concurs. Then we get the syndrome 'They were so good to me'. We have the 'There, there' approach to disability, when the employer says, 'Don't worry, we'll look after you', and there follows a redundancy notice with quite generous terms. The truth is that in many cases, perhaps a majority of cases, with the aid of retraining and technology the disability can quite easily be compensated. You only have to develop a bit of strain in your wrists when you have been sitting at the computer keyboard all day for the thought to flash through your mind, 'I'm getting old. I can't do it anymore. I'm no good.' Again, the truth is that with an adaptation of the keyboard which costs next to nothing, the pain and strain may well disappear and competence and confidence quickly return. The skill and experience of a useful employee have been preserved and a person's life has been saved from sadness.[11]

Once, when travelling in Australia, I was asked to meet a very able man who was working in one of the government departments. I went to his office, which was well organized, and his staff were hurrying in and out dealing with messages and making coffee. As we talked, he told me that he had handed in his notice. When I asked why, he explained, with some hesitancy, that he had an irreversible ophthalmological condition and faced the prospect of losing his sight. The diagnosis had been confirmed and his sight already showed signs of deterioration, so he had offered his resignation and his employers, in sympathetic gratitude for his past services, had accepted it with regret. The intelligence, experience, management skills and creativity of this man were lost to society, and all for nothing, since it would have been possible for him to have continued in his work as a completely blind person.

It all depends what your work is. If you are collecting the garbage on the city dust-cart, sight is necessary (although it would not surprise me to receive an indignant letter from the Confederation of Blind Garbage Collectors), and if you are flying a jumbo jet it would be difficult to maintain the confidence of your passengers and crew if you were blind. By the way, when one of my children recently visited the flight deck of a Boeing 727 he came back amazed at how small the windows were. He had expected huge vistas of glass so that the pilots could see all around. With modern radar and other technology, the sight of the pilot moment by moment is certainly less important. Sight is more necessary for reading the instruments than for flying the plane.

However, if you are in a management position, blindness is often not much of a hindrance. When it is a matter of intelligence, planning, decision-making, developing policies and evaluating them and so on, a highly motivated and organized blind person can be extremely effective. What matters is judgement, efficiency and creativity, not eyes.

Tobit is a typical example of someone whose blindness was quickly interpreted by him as a mark of God's disfavour. 'And now your judgements are true in exacting penalty from me for my sins. For we have not kept your commandments' (Tob. 3.5).

In spite of all this, blindness is not always associated with punishment or ridicule. There is a failure of sight which is due to excessive longing, a yearning after the presence of God in which the eyes as well as the heart may fail. 'My eyes fail with watching for your promise; I ask, "When will you comfort me?"' (Ps. 119.82). And later in the same psalm, 'My eyes fail from watching for your salvation, and for the fulfilment of your righteous promise' (v. 123).

3

Sighted Bible/sighted God

The Bible was written by sighted people

It is not surprising that the Bible was written by sighted people. However, blind readers of the Bible need to be aware of this fact. Otherwise, blind and partially sighted readers are likely to find themselves alienated from the Bible without understanding why. When it is recognized that the Bible was written by and for sighted people (and after all, they are the vast majority in any society), it can be understood that this is not a permanent or particularly significant aspect of the message of the Bible. It is just the way that it was unconsciously adapted by the sighted people who wrote it.

Let us begin with the common image of hiding one's face from someone. 'Do not hide your face from your servant, for I am in distress' (Ps. 69.17). The idea of hiding one's face is a sighted person's way of describing displeasure or shame. The act of reading in the ancient world was always visual. Of course, people read aloud while others listened, but there were no computers, no tape recorders and no Braille. This is why, when the psalmist is speaking about reading, he or she says, 'Open my eyes, so that I may behold wondrous things out of your law' (Ps. 119.18). The use of the idea of opening the eyes to indicate understanding is very common in the Bible. The implication is that blindness is a state of ignorance and insensitivity. In the same way, understanding is symbolized by light. 'The unfolding of your words gives light; it imparts understanding to the simple' (Ps. 119.130), 'The light of the eyes rejoices the heart, and good news refreshes the body' (Prov. 15.30). An unusual visual image is found in Prov. 27:19, 'Just as water reflects the face, so one human heart reflects another.' Sometimes the eye is used to indicate the whole person. 'The eye that mocks a father and scorns to obey a mother will be pecked out by the ravens of the valley and eaten by the vultures' (Prov. 30.17).

A particularly vivid example of sighted prejudice is to be found in Eccles. 1.12–13: 'So I turned to consider wisdom and madness and folly . . . Then I saw that wisdom excels folly as light excels darkness. The wise have eyes in their head, but the fools walk in darkness.' We can only wonder whether, as thousands of sighted people have read these verses down the centuries, it has occurred to any that they are hurtful to blind people. '[Wisdom] is more beautiful than the sun, and excels every constellation of the stars. Compared with the light she is found to be superior, for it is succeeded by the night, but against wisdom evil does not prevail' (Wisd. 7.29–30).

In Sirach one finds a good example of how sighted people appraise each other. 'A person is known by his appearance, and a sensible person is known when first met, face to face. A person's attire and hearty laughter, and the way he walks, show what he is' (Sir. 19.29–30). In the opinion of Ben Sirach, it would be impossible for a blind person to form a view about anything or make any judgements, hence 'favours and gifts blind the eyes of the wise; like a muzzle on the mouth, they stop reproofs' (Sir. 20.29). In Sirach 23 we have a description of adultery, again offered exclusively from the sighted person's point of view. Perhaps blind people never committed adultery. Perhaps they never dared to, in case they got caught, whereas sighted people could do what they liked in the darkness.

> The one who sins against his marriage bed
>   says to himself, 'Who can see me?
> Darkness surrounds me, the walls hide me,
>   and no one sees me. Why should I worry?

The Most High will not remember sins.'
His fear is confined to human eyes,
    and he does not realize that the eyes of the Lord
    are ten thousand times brighter than the sun;
they look upon every aspect of human behaviour
    and see into hidden corners.

(Sir. 23.18–19)

An interesting example of the different points of view between God and the biblical authors is found in the story of the call of David the shepherd boy. Samuel was inspecting the sons of Jesse, since he had been told that one of them was to be anointed as the future king. When the oldest came in,

the Lord said to Samuel, 'Do not look on his appearance or on the height of his stature, because I have rejected him; for the Lord does not see as mortals see; they look on the outward appearance, but the Lord looks on the heart.' (I Sam. 16.7)

However, when the shepherd boy is called down from the hills to be inspected, the narrator tells us that David was handsome and had beautiful eyes (v. 12). This, however, is the very sort of thing that the Lord has said is of no importance, and Samuel is warned against being influenced by such things. There is an inconsistency in the story, which we can understand if we remember that it is being written by a sighted person who has not altogether understood the nature of God as being beyond sighted people's preferences.

Blindness as an obstacle

You shall not revile the deaf or put a stumbling block before the blind; you shall fear your God: I am the Lord. (Lev. 19.14)

The Lord spoke to Moses, saying: Speak to Aaron and say:
No one of your offspring throughout their generations who
has a blemish may approach to offer the food of his God.
For no one who has a blemish shall draw near, one who is
blind or lame, or one who has a mutilated face or a limb
too long, or a man who has a broken foot or a broken hand,
or a hunchback, or a dwarf, or a man with a blemish in his
eyes or an itching disease or scabs or crushed testicles. No
descendant of Aaron the priest who has a blemish shall come
near to offer the Lord's offerings by fire; since he has a
blemish, he shall not come near to offer the food of his God.
He may eat the food of his God, of the most holy as well
as of the holy. But he shall not come near the curtain or
approach the altar, because he has a blemish, that he may
not profane my sanctuaries; for I am the Lord; I sanctify
them. (Lev. 21. 16–23)

There is a striking contrast between these two quotations. In
the first place, we see that the fear of God and the knowledge
of God shall prevent anyone from putting an obstacle in the
path of deaf or blind people. On the other hand, the same fear
of God should prevent anyone from allowing a blind person
(or someone with any kind of disability) from ministering to
God in the temple. The same Lord who commands people
not to place an obstacle before the blind finds that the blind
themselves are an obstacle in God's worship. The Lord seems
to have the same kind of ambivalent attitude towards disabled
people as is found in society as a whole. They are not to be
impeded, but they are not to be given responsibility either.
They are not to be hindered and they are not to be helped.
The verse says nothing about guiding blind people, only about
not tripping them up. They can wander along as they will,
provided that you do not maliciously stop them. It is only
when they try to approach the altar that you must stop them.
Then you must put an obstacle in the path of the blind person,
an obstacle which consists of nothing other than the command

of the Lord. Blind people may indeed eat, which prevents them
from serving.

The same prohibition applies to animals. Referring to the
animals offered in sacrifice, we read:

> When anyone offers a sacrifice ... to the Lord ... to be
> acceptable it must be perfect; there shall be no blemish in
> it. Anything blind, or injured, or maimed, or having a dis-
> charge or an itch or scabs – these you shall not offer to the
> Lord or put any of them on the altar as offerings by fire to
> the Lord. (Lev. 22.21f.)

This prohibition is also found in Deut. 15.21, where the animals that may be offered to the Lord in sacrifice are described:
'But if it has any defect – any serious defect, such as lameness
or blindness – you shall not sacrifice it to the Lord your God'.
As the following verse indicates, such animals could be eaten
but not sacrificed. They are good enough for the table but not
good enough for God. In Mal. 1.8 the reason for this is made
clear:

> When you offer blind animals in sacrifice, is that not wrong?
> And when you offer those that are lame or sick, is that not
> wrong? Try presenting that to your governor; will he be
> pleased with you, or show you favour? says the Lord of
> hosts.

The people are attacked for offering to God that which was
of no real value, animals they could not otherwise dispose of.
This would be an insult to God; you would be cheating God
by offering a blind animal just as you would be cheating someone in the market by trying to sell such a beast. 'Cursed be
the cheat who ... sacrifices to the Lord what is blemished; for
I am a great King, says the Lord of Hosts, and my name is
reverenced among the nations' (Mal. 1.14).

There are two assumptions behind these passages. First, it

is assumed that the disabled are useless. Just as you would not try to sell a defective animal, or give such a beast as a present to someone you respect, so a disabled person should not serve in the temple. That would be to fob God off with the second rate. It would be like someone offering for the ministry of the church who had already proved that he or she was incapable of doing anything else.

The other implication has to do with perfection. Remorselessly the passages hammer home the thought that the disabled person has a blemish. Such people are not like those who have come straight from the hand of the Creator. They do not express the perfection of the handiwork of God, and therefore embody the imperfections of a sinful world. The question of responsibility, of how the person came to be disabled, does not arise. No distinction is made between accident and disease. Such people cannot stand before God because God is perfect, and it would insult God's handiwork if that which deviates from it were to be presented right in front of God's own altar.

Such attitudes may seem somewhat primitive, but they are still with us today. This becomes clear when you listen to the stories of blind men and women who have sought ordination in the church. Jane Wallman recorded interviews with half a dozen such people, all of whom were finally ordained as priests in the Church of England.[12] They all tell stories of experiencing the same objection to their ministry. A priest or minister is meant to care for others, but a blind person needs caring for. How can you care for others when you yourself need care? This was the comment made again and again.

The implications of this question are rather startling. Apparently, only a person who does not need any care, someone who is completely independent, someone who has no need of the love and care of others, only such a person can offer pastoral help and friendship.

Not only do we still find the assumption that the blind minister requires caring for (one must not place an obstacle in the path of a blind person) and therefore cannot care for others (blind people are themselves obstacles), but the assumption about perfection also lives on. Although she was fully trained and prepared for ordination, Jane Wallman had difficulty in finding a bishop who would ordain her. The first bishop said she had a defect. A second bishop made a similar comment. Not until the principal of her theological college appealed to the Archbishop of Canterbury could a bishop be found to ordain her.

' "Cursed be anyone who misleads a blind person on the road." All the people shall say, "Amen",' (Duet. 27.18). This verse sums up the attitude of the Bible towards blind people. There is a preoccupation with problems of mobility, expressed in negative compassion. One is not required to lead but one may not mislead. Behind this apparent compassion, however, lies a deep failure to offer acceptance and inclusion.

God is sighted

He who formed the eye, does he not see? (Ps. 94.9)

Do you have eyes of flesh? Do you see as humans see? (Job 10.4)

The cause must be at least as great as its effect. Since created beings have the power of sight, that power must be present in the Creator. Usually, this power of sight is spiritualized. The eyes of God are not like human eyes, but because of the general parallel between sight and knowledge, God who is all-knowing must be all-seeing. The analogy between sight, light and knowledge, which runs not only through the Bible but through most sighted people's literature, is so compelling, so obvious, that it is inevitable to imagine God as being sighted. Sometimes the identity of seeing and knowing is expressed in a completely taken-for-granted manner. When God had finished creating the earth, 'God saw everything that he had made, and indeed, it was very good' (Gen. 1.31) and 'The Lord saw that the wickedness of humankind was great in the earth, and that every inclination of the thoughts of their hearts was only evil continually' (Gen. 6.5).

At other times, sight is attributed to God in a more positional sense. God has to be in a position where God can see. In these cases, God is regarded as a sighted person in a more literal sense. 'The Lord came down to see the city and the tower, which mortals had built' (Gen. 11.5). When Solomon dedicates the temple, he prays to God, 'May your eyes be open day and night toward this house, the place where you promised to set your name ... let your eyes be open and your ears attentive to prayer from this place' (II Chron. 6.20, 40).

At other times the metaphor is extended, so that the eyes of God are represented as being more or less detached from God's body, in order to rove throughout the world. 'For the eyes of the Lord range throughout the entire earth' (II Chron. 16.9); 'The eyes of the Lord are in every place, keeping watch on the evil and the good' (Prov. 15.3). In Jer. 32.19, God is 'great in counsel and mighty in deed; whose eyes are open to all the ways of mortals, rewarding all according to their ways'.

Because of God's keen eyesight, it is impossible to hide from God.

> Though they dig into Sheol,
>> from there shall my hand take them;
> though they climb up to heaven,
>> from there I will bring them down.
> Though they hide themselves on the top of Carmel,
>> from there I will search out and take them;
> and though they hide from my sight at the bottom of the
> sea,
>> there I will command the sea-serpent, and it shall bite
> them . . .
> I will fix my eyes on them
>> for harm and not for good.

(Amos 9.2–4)

The idea that God is sighted is used poetically to emphasize the impossibility of evading God. Perhaps there are circumstances in which God cannot quite see you, but still God has ways of getting at you. God may not quite be able to see you at the bottom of the sea, perhaps, but it does not matter because he can command the serpent and it will get you. Another example is found in Job.

> 'Is not God high in the heavens?
> See the highest stars, how lofty they are!
> Therefore you say, "What does God know?
> Can [God] judge through the deep darkness?
> Thick clouds enwrap [God], so that [God] does not see,
> And [God] walks on the dome of heaven.'
> (Job 22.12–14)

God is very high. Perhaps God cannot see quite as far as where we are. Anyway, God is supposed to be surrounded by thick clouds of darkness, so God will not be able to see through them, and God is separated from us by the dome of heaven upon which God walks. These are poetic devices in which the limits of literal sight are applied ironically to God.

In spite of this general description of God as sighted, there is also an awareness in the Bible that this description of God is inadequate and even misleading. When Samuel the prophet and seer was deliberating about which of the sons of Jesse would be chosen as the future king, 'the Lord said to Samuel, "Do not look on his appearance or on the height of his stature ... for the Lord does not see as mortals see; they look on the outward appearance, but the Lord looks on the heart"' (I Sam. 16.7).

Another vivid example of how the idea that God is a seeing God must be qualified is found in the Sermon on the Mount. Jesus tells his listeners to make sure that when they give to people in need, they do it secretly, 'And your Father who sees in secret will reward you' (Matt. 6.4). The idea of one who sees in secret, that is, one whose vision penetrates into places where no human eye can perceive, is referred to even more vividly in the verses which follow. 'But whenever you pray, go into your room and shut the door and pray to your Father who is in secret.' You pray secretly to a secret Father. Sight is so public. Sight works best in large spaces where there is plenty of scope for detail and distance . . . 'And your Father, who sees in secret, will reward you' (v. 6). What does it mean to see in secret? This is a paradoxical seeing, a seeing of that which is hidden from normal sight.

The God of the Bible was, therefore, a sighted God but many of the biblical authors were aware of the limits of this language. They recognized that sight had its limitations and defects. Therefore the idea of God as a sighted God must be qualified. God is at least sighted and, when understood more perfectly, God is beyond sight and blindness.

Visual visions

> Raise your eyes now, and look from the place where you are, northward and southward and eastward and westward; for all the land that you see I will give to you and to your offspring forever. (Gen. 13.14–15)

Many of the revelations and visions of the Bible are expressed in terms which only a sighted person could appreciate. The promise of God to Abraham about the land which his descendants would inherit is a case in point. Later on, 'he brought him outside and said "Look toward heaven and count the stars, if you are able to count them." Then he said to him "So shall your descendants be"' (Gen. 15.5).

When Sarah cast out her handmaiden Hagar, the angel of the Lord visited Hagar in the desert. Hagar named the Lord who spoke to her 'El-roi' (a God of seeing), for she said, 'Have I really seen God, and remained alive after seeing him?' (Gen. 16.13). Here God is regarded almost as the patron deity of sight. God saw her and was seen by her.

A more specifically visual account of a divine revelation is given in Exodus 24. Moses, Aaron and seventy leaders of the people had gone up the mountain, 'and they saw the God of Israel. Under his feet there was something like a pavement of sapphire stone, like the very heaven for clearness ... they beheld God, and they ate and drank' (Ex. 24.10–11). The description is confined to the pavement upon which God sat rather than God's own person, nevertheless the people said that they had seen God. A striking feature of this vision is not really that they saw God, but that what they saw was so predominantly visual. At a later point in the story, Moses reminds God of how the Egyptians have heard 'that you, O Lord, are in the midst of this people; for you, O Lord, are seen face to face' (Num. 14.14).

Another example of a vision which is not only visual but incorporates the visual within it is to be found in Ezekiel. This is the great vision of the wheels, much loved by the writers of science fiction. The four wheels each had rims and spokes, and their rims were 'full of eyes all around ... Like the bow in a cloud on a rainy day, such was the appearance of the splendour all around' (Ezek. 1.18, 28). The vision is also referred to in Ezekiel 10, where we read that 'Their entire body, their rims, their spokes, their wings and the wheels ... were full of eyes all around' (Ezek. 10.12).

A vision which appears to be entirely visual is found in II Kings 3. The armies of Israel and Judah were trapped in the desert without water and the Maobite army was advancing towards them. In response to a prophetic prayer from Elisha, pools of water appeared in the desert and 'When they rose early in the morning, and the sun shone upon the water, the Moabites saw the water opposite them as red as blood' (v. 22); they concluded that the Israelite armies had been slaughtering each other and withdrew. In the early morning, the vision of the red blood must have seemed eerie indeed, but this was a vision experienced in complete silence.

On the other hand, many of the visions and religious experiences reported in the Bible do have aural elements. There is little visual content in the experience which Elijah had, hiding on the mountaintop. He would have heard the sound of the wind and the crackling of the fire and the earthquake, and even when he went to the mouth of the cave, he covered his face with his tunic (I Kings 19.11–13). The account of his being taken up into heaven in a chariot drawn by fiery horses is more visual, but even then one would have heard the sound of the whirlwind, and perhaps the galloping of the heavenly horses (II Kings 2.11). Ezekiel's vision of the wings, although powerfully visual, contains a lot which a blind person could appreciate. The wings of the living creatures made a sound 'like . . . mighty waters, like the thunder of the Almighty, a sound of tumult like the sound of an army' (Ezek. 1.24). This reminds me of the powerful experience of a Tornado fighter plane passing overhead. Since the plane is travelling faster than the speed of sound, you hear it before you see it. First comes the sound, a terrible roar that rushes to an ear-splitting climax and is gone. By the time a sighted person glances up, the aircraft is already in the distance. It also reminds me of the preparations for the G8 Summit meeting in Birmingham in May 1998. A few days before, as I was working in my office on the third floor of the Education Building in the early evening, my work with my assistant was interrupted by an approaching roaring sound from outside the window. At first I thought it must be a Jumbo Jet landing at Birmingham International Airport, but then I realized that its progress was too slow. It came on steadily, implacably getting louder and louder. Then whatever it was passed right over my building with an oppressive, shattering heaviness and went on its way. By that time my sighted assistant had leapt to his feet and run to the window: two large, fully armed American helicopters were circling around the area, presumably on security duty. This is what it must have been like when Ezekiel heard the grinding roar of the wheels and the immense thunder of the heavenly wings.

You had to see the snake

> Whenever a serpent bit someone, that person would look at the serpent of bronze and live. (Num. 21.9)

Wandering through the wilderness, the people grow impatient and complain to Moses. 'Why have you brought us up out of Egypt just to die here in the desert?' they say. 'There is no food here and no water and as for this manna that keeps falling from heaven every morning and the quails that come in the evening, we are completely sick and tired of eating them!' Just then lots of poisonous snakes come slithering into the camp. The people feel so guilty for complaining that they naturally assume God is sending the snakes. People start to scream and run. Parents snatch their children up in their arms and others try to get inside their tents, hoping the snakes will not follow them. There are probably a few blind people. It takes them a few seconds to realize what is happening. They hear people shouting 'Snakes! Run for your lives!', but blind people never know which way to run. Some run this way and that, right into a pile of snakes. The best thing is probably to climb on the back of a mule, but can a blind person find a mule in time? This is probably not the sort of occasion when a sighted person would say to a hesitating blind person, 'Where are you trying to get to? Can I help you?'

'Oh, thank you, I'm just trying to find a mule so I can climb on its back and get away from all these snakes.'

'Sorry mate, all the mules seem to have bolted and run. Try climbing up that tent post over there.'

By this time, there are shrieks and groans from dying people, lying on the ground with snakes still crawling over them. Some of the people have gathered around Moses and are demanding that he should do something. They say they are sorry they grumbled so much, and they certainly mean it. Moses has a sudden inspiration which really seems to come directly from God. 'Make a big model serpent and stick it up on a pole.

Anyone who looks at the serpent will live.' In the next few minutes, the Israelite bronzesmiths break their own personal best for serpent making. Soon the big curving metal snake is strung up on a pole in the middle of the camp. Everyone who looks upon the bronze snake lives.

But what do the blind people do?

See the star

> We observed his star at its rising, and have come to pay him homage. (Matt. 2.2)

Whereas in Luke's infancy narrative there are songs and an angelic choir (Luke 2.13), the story as presented by Matthew has more material of a visual kind. The wise men came to enquire about the birth of Jesus from King Herod because they had seen a star. When they had heard the advice of Herod, 'they set out; and there, ahead of them, went the star that they had seen at its rising, until it stopped over the place where the child was. When they saw that the star had stopped, they were overwhelmed with joy' (Matt. 2.9–10). When they entered the house, 'they saw the child with Mary his mother' (v. 11).

It is always difficult greeting babies when you cannot see them. You have to be so careful as you cautiously stretch out your hand lest you make contact with the baby's nose and start a cry of alarm or, perhaps even worse, manage to prod the mother in some sensitive region. Of course, it is great to hold a little baby, and the smell and feel of such a young child is always delightful. I have had four children since I lost my sight and always carried my babies around, usually over my right shoulder, holding their ankles firmly with my left hand, leaving my right hand free to negotiate doors and walls or hold the cane. When going through a doorway, I would always place my hand slightly on the baby's head just to make sure that the baby didn't suddenly lift its head up and get a knock from the lintel. I did this over a period of at least ten years and never once dropped a baby, knocked its head on anything or caused it any harm, except once when, entering a building, some helpful sighted person opened the door towards me as I was approaching and, before I realized what was happening, I walked into the edge of the door with the baby. There was no harm done and the baby seemed more amused than annoyed. However, when it is not your baby and you are not holding it, contact is much more difficult. Sometimes the baby will stretch out its hand towards you, which is nice because you can locate the baby's hand and follow it up to its head and lightly touch its hair. The hair of a baby is amazingly fine and light, and I love the warm fragrance of the baby's head. If I had been one of those wise men, perhaps Mary would have held her baby up to me, realizing that I could not see him. Maybe I would have taken the baby in my arms, because Mary would trust me. Perhaps the baby would gurgle and stretch out a hand towards me. I could hold that little hand and follow that chubby arm up to his face. Maybe he would allow me to rest my hand for a moment gently on his brow and then run my fingers through his hair. He would gaze at me but I would not know if he was smiling. Would he understand? I would offer him my gifts – the myrrh and the frankincense, because of their rich fragrance. This is why I chose them, for him to smell. I would take the lids off the little jars and he would chuckle.

Feeling birds and bread

He saw the Spirit of God descending like a dove and alight-ing on him. (Matt. 3.16)

He could hardly have seen the dove actually alighting upon him; he must have felt it. When I was a boy in a small country town in Victoria, sometimes the magpies (the maggies, we called them) would dive at us during the nesting season. You hardly ever saw them coming. There was simply a sudden flurry of wings and a squawking and you just had time to get your satchel above your head and duck, and then it was gone. There were stories of children being scratched and cut by the attacking birds, and we treated them with great respect.

In 1996 I was with my son Thomas, then aged nearly sixteen, in the hills near Los Angeles. As we strolled around the grounds of our conference centre, there was a sudden rush of something diving to the earth and then a small animal screamed. It could not have been more than thirty or forty feet away from us. It was a bird of prey which had stooped upon a mouse or some such creature. The speed with which it dropped from the sky was such that you only heard it as it was about to grasp its victim. Then it was gone.

The nearest I have come to having a bird alight on me was some years ago, after I had lost my sight. The man next door was a pigeon-fancier. The children found an injured bird on the sloping roof of the university gymnasium and took it home to Mr Budd, who cared for it until it recovered. After that, he used to ask us in to admire his pigeons. One or two would fly up and stand on my shoulder, or he would tell me to hold out my hand and would place a pigeon on my outstretched palm.

Jesus would have felt the weight of the bird as it alighted on his shoulder. He would have sensed the warmth of the bird's body and then the motion as it gathered its wings and flew away.

A blind person can certainly appreciate all that, but what about the temptations? At first glance, so to speak, the account does seem to be rather visual. We normally suppose that the tempter pointed to the stones lying around in the desert and said to Jesus, 'Command these stones to become loaves of bread' (Matt. 4.3) and that when the devil placed Jesus on the pinnacle of the temple, it was the sight of the tiny people so far below which gave terror to the temptation to throw himself down. As to the third temptation, it seems clear that it was visual: 'The devil took him to a very high mountain and showed him all the kingdoms of the world and their splendour' (Matt. 4.8).

Maybe we should read this story differently. Imagine if Jesus were a blind person. He would probably have been holding some of the round, smooth, hot stones in his hand, turning them over and over and imagining that they were beautiful little warm bread rolls. It was then that the thought of turning the stones into bread came to him.

Although there are many things which people can give a blind person for presents, statues and models, drinking mugs and paper weights, there are few things more attractive than the feel of a stone in one's hand. Whether washed smooth by the ocean, or jagged where an ancient violence has struck it, the infinite variety and texture of small stones is a never-failing source of wonder. As for bread rolls, the fragrance and crunchiness when you break open one is rather exquisite. Perhaps something like that went through the mind of Jesus.

Then he was taken up to two high places, first on top of a building and then on top of a mountain. When you are blind, it is good to be up high. My room is on the third floor of my office block and is just high enough for the rustling in the tops of the nearby trees to be my daily companion. Below me and further out, I hear the sounds of the city, with considerable detail near at hand, but as the sound-horizon recedes it is a general deep roar of city noise. It is delightful to be even higher. On the top of the Empire State Building in New York, the street noise seems very far away and the helicopters that pass overhead seem a good deal closer. Of course, if it is glassed in, like the observation platforms on many tall buildings, it is not so good; but if it is only a wire mesh, as in the case of the Empire State Building, you feel the breeze blowing from a certain direction and it mingles with the sound of bird cries and the more distant sounds from the waterways. As for mountaintops, the first thing a blind person would notice is the coolness of the air, and then its movement. Sometimes the wind is strong, but the best thing is that the air is so wonderfully fresh and pure. The next thing you notice is the silence. Perhaps far off there might be a train, but that somehow heightens the sense of silence and distance. It was from such a place that Jesus was able to imagine all the empires of the world stretched out beneath him.

Was Paul partially-sighted?

It is possible that Paul never completely recovered from his blindness on the Damascus road. There are traces of this here and there in his letters. In Gal. 4.13–15 Paul writes:

> You know that it was because of a physical infirmity that I first announced the gospel to you; though my condition put you to the test, you did not scorn or despise me, but welcomed me as an angel of God, as Christ Jesus. What has become of the good will you felt? For I testify that, had it been possible, you would have torn out your eyes and given them to me.

Why would the Galatians want to give Paul their own eyes? From what we have seen of the image of blindness in the Hebrew Bible, it is not surprising that Paul should have expected the Galatians to scorn or despise him as a partially-sighted person. Indeed, to some extent Paul shared this negative attitude towards blind people. In his letter to the Romans (2.19–20) he addresses the Jews at Rome, who were so proud of their ancient heritage and thought that they had so much to offer everyone: 'And if you are sure that you are a guide to the blind, a light to those who are in darkness, a corrector of the foolish, a teacher of children, having in the law the embodiment of knowledge and truth . . .'. Here, blindness is associated with foolishness, with being ignorant and needing to be taught, with being a child. These words could so easily have been written by someone who had himself been patronized and treated like a child because he needed to be guided from place to place. The Galatians, however, had not responded to Paul in this way. Rather than being like the angel in the book of Tobit, who guided the young and offered healing to the blind, the Galatians were so sympathetic that they turned the tables and treated Paul as if it was he who was the angel. Instead of attempting to be Jesus Christ to him and heal him, they treated him as if he were Jesus Christ, the healer.

At the end of the (dictated) letter to the Galatians, Paul takes up the pen to add his own personal message; the Galatians would have noticed the change in the handwriting. Like most visually handicapped people, he wrote in very large letters: 'See what large letters I am writing in my own hand' (Gal. 6.11). Paul's distinctive handwriting, due to his poor vision, was a well known feature of his signature.

There are several incidents in the book of Acts which support the view that Paul had limited sight. When he was brought before the Council in Jerusalem to give an account of himself, he had no sooner begun than the High Priest Ananias, who would have been wearing his full regalia on such a formal occasion, commanded that Paul should be struck on the mouth. Paul protested, saying, 'God will strike you, you whitewashed wall! Are you sitting there to judge me according to the law, and yet in violation of the law you order me to be struck?' (Acts 23.2). When the people around him said, 'Do you dare to insult God's high priest?' Paul quickly apologized with the words, 'I did not realize, brothers, that he was the high priest' (vv. 4, 5). How could Paul not know? Surely he was familiar with the regalia of the High Priest? Is it possible that he saw only a blur of whiteness, among several others, and hence his remark, 'You whitewashed wall'?

When Paul's ship was wrecked on the coast of Malta and the friendly inhabitants were preparing a fire to warm the party, dripping wet from the sea, 'Paul had gathered a bundle of brushwood and was putting it on the fire, when a viper, driven out by the heat, fastened itself on his hand' (Acts 28.3). It seems that Paul had enough sight to gather up the sticks but not enough to tell the difference between a stick and a snake.

Moreover, it took him a moment or two to realize what had happened:

> When the natives saw the creature hanging from his hand, they said to one another, 'This man must be a murderer; though he has escaped from the sea, justice has not allowed him to live.' He, however, shook off the creature into the fire and suffered no harm. (vv. 4, 5)

The Maltese noticed the snake before Paul did.

Nobody is more sensitive about not being blind than a partially-sighted person. This is, perhaps, the reason why Paul minimized his temporary blindness when defending himself to the Jews (Acts 22.11; see p. 54 above), explaining that he could not see 'because of the brightness of that light'. He went on to explain how, because of the ministry of Ananias, he had received his sight again, although there is some ambiguity about the expression; but when he is defending himself before King Agrippa any reference to his sight having been restored disappears altogether (Acts 26). At the same time, the brightness of the vision is heightened. It is 'brighter than the sun' (Acts 26.13). It is perfectly possible, then, that Paul did have rather poor sight, and used to explain it by reference to the fact that he had been semi-blinded by gazing at the light, brighter than the sun.

If we consider the metaphors of light and darkness as used by Paul in his letters, or by those in his circle, we find that they are less stark than in the Gospel of John. Let us take, for example, the discussion about light and darkness in Eph. 5.8–14:

> For once you were darkness, but now in the Lord you are light. Live as children of light – for the fruit of the light is found in all that is good and right and true. Try to find out what is pleasing to the Lord. Take no part in the unfruitful works of darkness, but instead expose them. For it is

shameful even to mention what such people do secretly; but everything exposed by the light becomes visible, for everything that becomes visible is light. Therefore it says, 'Sleeper, awake! Rise from the dead, and Christ will shine on you.'

Contrast that with John 9:39–41:

Jesus said, 'I came into this world for judgement so that those that do not see may see, and those that do see may become blind.' Some of the Pharisees near him heard this and said to him, 'Surely we are not blind, are we?' Jesus said to them, 'If you were blind, you would not have sin. But now that you say, "We see," your sin remains.'

The passage from John is typical of a sighted person's view of blindness. It is absolute: either you are blind or you are sighted, in light or in darkness. The passage in Ephesians, on the other hand, is typical of the way in which a partially-sighted person would look at the world. There is no reference to blindness. Although darkness is mentioned as the opposite of light, it is not in the context of blindness and seeing but in the context of things becoming visible or invisible. 'Everything exposed by the light becomes visible' (v. 13). Here we see the experience of a partially-sighted person who, by lighting a torch, opening wide the door, or waiting until the sun breaks through, is able to see things which previously were hidden. As the objects become visible with the increasing light, the partially-sighted person would indeed exclaim, 'Everything that is visible is light!' Christ is that light which, shining upon us as it shone around Paul on the Damascus road, brings the invisible into clarity. The image of the fruit of light and the fruit of darkness suggests that you are trying to pick a fruit from a tree as the evening light is fading. It becomes too dark and the fruit becomes invisible. When the morning light breaks again, however, you can go out into your garden and now the fruit has become visible. In comparison, the passage in John appears stark and bleak. Blindness is total.

In Eph. 1.18 the apostle speaks of 'having the eyes of your hearts enlightened'. Once again, the contrast is not between sheer blindness and absolute sight but the idea of an enlightening process in which vision becomes functional again. The interest in 'things visible and invisible' is found again in Col. 1.16, where Paul says, speaking of Christ, 'for in him all things in heaven and on earth were created, things visible and invisible'.

It is characteristic of the experience of a partially-sighted person that one becomes acutely conscious of the limits of vision itself. As your own vision becomes restricted, the fallible and potentially dangerous nature of sight dawns upon you. So it is natural that Paul should have said that we look not to the things which are seen, but to the things which are unseen, for 'what can be seen is temporary, but what cannot be seen is eternal' (II Cor. 4.18). When you are partially sighted, you learn that what you have to look out for is not what you can see, but what you cannot see. Yes, indeed, I see the single point of light from that street light, but it throws no light on anything else. It shows me where to go, but it does not relieve me of the dangerous possibilities that before I get there, there will be some steps, a rosebed or even a dangerous drop. In addition, it is the unseen things that are most beautiful and therefore most tantalizing. I see that white blob which is your face, or the dark shape of the outline of your body as you are more or less silhouetted against the window, but I cannot make out your expression. Are you smiling or are you sneering? Are you gazing at me with interest or looking away in boredom? The outline of your shadow does not tell me if you are beautiful or not. Are you beautiful? I could tell that if I came closer and peered at you, but I do not dare. Until then, what is unseen is more interesting that what is seen.

A partially-sighted person learns to call upon senses other than sight, which is fluctuating and unreliable. However sensitive your awareness of space might become, however familiar you may be with the way, there remains an element of risk, 'for we walk by faith, not by sight' (II Cor. 5.7).

Another feature of the language of Paul which is consistent with a partially-sighted person's outlook on the world is his use of the idea of a veil which covers the mind.

> And even if our gospel is veiled, it is veiled to those who are perishing. In their case the god of this world has blinded the minds of the unbelievers, to keep them from seeing the light of the gospel of the glory of Christ, who is the image of God. (II Cor. 4.3–4)

This idea of a veil suggests the way the world looks to certain kinds of visual impairment. In my own case of retinal detachment, the world was seen through a deep, quivering green and yellow jelly. Every time the eye moved, the sea or ocean quivered and wobbled until it settled down. Colours were muted and edges lost their sharpness. It was like being in a cave below the surface of the sea. There were dark corners, shadowy recesses, but when the light fell upon them there was a brighter, yellowy sort of appearance. When I had cataracts as a child, it was quite different. Then it was like a grey mist, gradually becoming more dense. People would come out of the mist, bright colours would be veiled until even my hand grew dim as I extended it further away from my body. Finally, it became an impenetrable fog, turned into a dazzling opaque whiteness in the sunshine. The first thing I saw when the bandages were removed after the cataract operations was the edge of a door as it moved towards me. Someone was entering the room. The edge of the door was wonderfully sharp and clear; I had almost forgotten that there were such straight lines, such delightful movements, such wonderful colours.

> For it is the God who said, 'Let light shine out of darkness', who has shone in our hearts to give the light of the know-

ledge of the glory of God in the face of Jesus Christ. But we have this treasure in clay jars, so that it may be made clear that this extraordinary power belongs to God and does not come from us. (II Cor. 4.6–7)

A partially-sighted person does indeed become highly conscious of the beauty of light, and of perceiving this light as it were 'in a mirror, dimly' (I Cor. 13.12) and in a 'clay jar'.

So we do not lose heart. Even though our outer nature is wasting away, our inner nature is being renewed day by day. For this slight momentary affliction is preparing us for an eternal weight of glory beyond all measure, because we look not at what can be seen but at what cannot be seen. (II Cor. 4.16–18)

As my sight deteriorated, I found that I became nervous in the Education Building at night. Any large building, I suppose, can be a bit spooky when isolated at night. For a partially-sighted person this effect is heightened. Straining not only through the gloom toward the light switch, but also through the distortions of my sight itself, I became aware of shadows, deep recesses of darkness, and the possibility of an unknown presence. When I was a sighted person in Cambridge years ago, I would sometimes be alone in my college during the summer months when all the other students had gone to their homes. I was an overseas student and allowed to stay there. I would turn on the lights along the corridor and the stairs until I came to my own corridor. At my end it was lit by the switch I had just turned on, but at the far end of the corridor it was plunged in darkness. I would always walk into this darkness and switch on the light at the far end of the corridor. Then I would return to my room. At least I would know if anyone entered my corridor. As a partially-sighted person, that desire to know what was in the dark and who might be hiding in the shadows grew stronger. However, when I became completely blind, fear came to an end. I was no longer afraid of the building at night, since it was always the same for me, night or day. The only factor was whether people were around or not. The experience of the hidden unknown, the way that a partially-sighted person strains to see, all that went.

It is impossible to say whether Paul was partially sighted or not. However, a partially-sighted person reading his letters can certainly feel a sense of communion with Paul. People in the ancient world saw their reflections not in the clarity of the modern mirror, but in the dim reflection provided by pieces of beaten and polished metal. 'For now we see in a mirror, dimly, but then we will see face to face. Now I know only in part; then I will know fully, even as I have been fully known' (I Cor. 13.12).

Sex and sight

They have eyes full of adultery, insatiable for sin. (II Peter 2.14)

There is a close connection in the Bible between sight and sex. Peter describes wicked people as having 'eyes full of adultery', which seems to be influenced by the saying attributed to Jesus in Matt. 5.28, 'everyone who looks at a woman with lust has already committed adultery with her in his heart'. The fact that this is immediately followed by the saying about plucking out your eye if it offends you suggests that taking out the eyes is similar to castration. A blind man, we are told, is like a castrated man: he is not capable of sexual arousal. Similarly, the implication of the verse from II Peter is that without eyes one cannot be 'full of adultery'.

These ideas are emphasized in I John 2.16: 'For all that is in the world – the desire of the flesh, the desire of the eyes, the pride in riches – comes not from the Father but from the world.' This recalls the story in Genesis 3 of how, when Eve saw that the fruit looked good, she desired it; and, in Genesis

6, the story about how 'the sons of God saw that they [the daughters of men] were fair' (v. 2). It always seems to be one's eyes that lead one into sin. Job challenges God to say whether 'I have walked with falsehood, and my foot has hurried to deceit . . . if my step has turned aside from the way, and my heart has followed my eyes' (Job 31.5, 7). Accordingly, Job assures us, 'I have made a covenant with my eyes; how then could I look upon a virgin?' (Job 31.1). It is because of this close link between sight and sexual desire that the proverb says, 'Sheol and Abaddon are never satisfied, and human eyes are never satisfied' (Prov. 27.20).

Not only is this link between sex and seeing stated directly or indirectly in these and other passages, but the hint is also present in a number of stories from both classical and biblical literature. Oedipus inflicted blindness upon himself because he had unwittingly made love to his mother. It was when the Sodomites were knocking on the door of Lot's house in order to abuse Lot's angelic guests that they were smitten with blindness (Gen. 19.4–11). David was walking on the palace roof when he saw the beautiful Bathsheba having a bath in the garden next door (II Sam. 11.2). Samson's blindness is also associated with his sexual promiscuity (Judges 16). In the body-symbolism of much folk literature there is a connection between the eyeballs and the testicles, which probably represents the biological connection between sight and sex in the male of the human species. What you could not see, you would not desire, and what you did not desire you would not chase or hunt, and what you did not hunt you would not seize, and what you could not seize you would not have intercourse with.

What does all this say to blind people? Can one not be aroused by a beautiful, sexy voice just as much as by the sight of a beautiful person? This is certainly true, but perhaps it is also true that a difference remains. The word pornography suggests pictures. It is sex made graphic. Naturally, there are pornographic books which are not illustrated, but in spite of this there is certainly a strong connection between pornography and sight. The human voice can be erotic because it suggests the whole personality. The sight of the human body can be separated from the personality as a whole because of the objectivity of sight. The voice invites one to conversation and conversation sets up relationships which may indeed be highly erotic, but the sight, whether in actuality or in picture-form, of the naked human body can be pornographic because it makes possible the separation of physical sexuality from the emotional and intellectual mutuality of speech. It is some such reasoning as this which lies behind the belief that blind people are sexually pure.

After a busy day of lecturing in Montreal, my colleague and I came back to our hotel late in the evening, tired and hungry. We rang room service and asked for chicken, chips and beer. While we were waiting for the food, my colleague inspected the television set. On the top was a panel divided into squares, so smooth that it was impossible for a blind person to tell one from the next. Each square had a number on it, presumably of a film. At random, we pressed a certain number and, having watched for a few minutes, my colleague told me that this was a pornographic movie. At that moment, the food and drink arrived. We decided to switch channels, only to discover it was impossible to dislodge the pornographic film. The sound track was minimal and, apart from the background music and an occasional grunt, I could make nothing of it, but my colleague let out a guffaw or two so I gathered it was not too bad. When we went to pay our bill the following morning, we found to our consternation that the film, together with its title (which was something like 'The Sweet Sins of Sexy Suzy'), was marked up on our account, which we were to sign and send to the Montreal Education Authority. We took the bill from the receptionist, sat down in a couple of remote armchairs and discussed the situation. To ask for a new bill with the offending item deleted would only draw attention to ourselves. We were flying out to Calgary that same day anyway, so who cared? We went back to the counter with the bill and I signed it.

Pornographic films of this kind really do mean very little to a blind person, but that does not mean that you become less human. You become hungry, sooner or later, even if you cannot see the chickens roasting in the window or the pizzas being made in the kitchen. Hunger is internal. You are aware of the feeling even if you cannot see the object which would satisfy it. The same is true of sexual desire. Once again, blindness presents us with a strange paradox. On the one hand, because blind people work by mutual attraction and personality rather than by immediate appearance, there is a sense in which the sexual relationships of blind people must be more personal and more intimate. On the other hand, because the need which you feel in your body is less discriminating towards its object, it is easy for blind people to become more or less undiscriminating. One is, at the same time, both more refined and more basic, both more delicately sensitive and more fundamentally driven by one's physical nature.

To emphasize the connection between sight and sex is not helpful to either the blind or the sighted. To sighted people, it suggests a kind of guilt in seeing, a guilt which denies the natural pleasure to human beings which comes from gazing at each other. To blind people, it suggests a deprivation leading to a purity which they do not feel and do not want. Indeed, since blindness can be rather an isolating condition, the need of blind people for intimacy is just as great if not greater. The truth is that human beings, whether blind or sighted, need each other. That need is most fully expressed and most deeply satisfied if intimacy is associated with mutual trust and love.

4

Metaphor and paradox

Blindness as a metaphor

> You must not distort justice . . . you must not accept bribes, for a bribe blinds the eyes of the wise and subverts the cause of those who are in the right. (Deut. 16.19)

This is one of the earliest occurrences of blindness as a metaphor for corruption, wickedness and sin, a metaphor which runs through many books of the Bible and which has caused untold distress to blind people. In the Wisdom of Solomon there is a meditation upon the wicked who are planning to destroy the righteous. 'Thus they reasoned, but they were led astray, for their wickedness blinded them' (Wisd. 2.21). God frustrates the plans of wicked people:

> He frustrates the devices of the crafty,
>> so that their hands achieve no success.
> He takes the wise in their own craftiness;
>> and the schemes of the wily are brought to a quick end.
> They meet with darkness in the daytime,
>> and grope at noonday as in the night.
>> (Job 5.12f.)

Here we see why blindness was thought to be such an appropriate metaphor for wickedness. Sighted people often find blind people fascinating because of their mobility problems. If you have not got a blind person within your immediate family circle, it is only in the street or on the road that you are likely to encounter one. In such a context, blindness becomes extremely visible, and the way that blind people walk has made a deep impression upon the imagination of sighted people. The use of the hands to assist the feet in mobility gives sighted people the impression that the blind are groping. They are, as we say, 'feeling their way forward', step by step. Of course, we are speaking of the days before there was a white cane, but although the white cane and the guide dog make it unnecessary for blind people to use their hands to feel their way forward, the swinging motion of the cane has almost become the symbol of blindness and the guide dog is also a very familiar image of blind people. Because blind people often walk hesitantly, especially without a dog or a white cane, they remind sighted people of those who have morally lost their way, whose path is devious.

Sometimes the metaphor of blindness is drawn out at considerable length. When Isaiah says that the enemies of Jerusalem will conquer the city, because of the unfaithfulness and wickedness of its inhabitants, he uses the image of the blind sentry. 'Israel's sentinels are blind, they are all without knowledge; they are all silent dogs that cannot bark; dreaming, lying down, loving to slumber' (Isa. 56.10). Blindness is the same as lack of knowledge. A blind person is like a watchdog that cannot bark, or like sleeping sentries. The punishment that will come upon the inhabitants of Jerusalem is the blindness which their lack of understanding so easily suggests to the prophet.

> Therefore justice is far from us,
>   and righteousness does not reach us;
> we wait for light, and lo! there is darkness;
>   and for brightness, but we walk in gloom.
> We grope like the blind along a wall,
>   groping like those who have no eyes;
> we stumble at noon as in the twilight;

among the vigorous as though we were dead . . .
For our transgressions before you are many.

(Isa. 59.9–10, 12)

Here we see how the natural tendency of blind people to put out a hand, not so much to steady themselves as to make sure of their exact position, is taken as a parable of sinfulness. Blind people like to have a hand on the railing; they like the clarity of a nice, smooth wall to walk beside. Sighted people use their eyes to tell where they are and blind people use their hands. This is quite natural and would cause no comment – except that sighted people can see blind people doing it and this fascinates and alarms them. What is so natural to the people in one world is so unnatural to those in another, and so the world of sight misunderstands the world of blindness.

The prophet Zephaniah has the same fascination which how blind people walk. When he is describing the day of the Lord, the day of judgement, he says that God will 'bring such distress upon people that they shall walk like the blind; because they have sinned against the Lord, their blood shall be poured out like dust' (Zeph. 1.17). Since walking like a blind person was a threatened judgement of God, it was only too easy to believe that those who already walked in this way were already judged by God. So blind people became metaphors of sinfulness.

It is Isaiah who has the heaviest responsibility for carrying forward the metaphor of blindness into the New Testament. Following the vision of God which he had in the temple, Isaiah was told:

'Go and say to this people:
"Keep listening, but do not comprehend;
keep looking, but do not understand."
Make the mind of this people dull,
    and stop their ears,
    and shut their eyes,
so that they may not look with their eyes

> and listen with their ears,
> and comprehend with their minds,
> and turn and be healed.'

(Isa. 6.9f.)

Jeremiah takes up the same thought: 'Hear this, O foolish and senseless people, who have eyes but do not see, who have ears, but do not hear' (Jer. 5.21).

One of the greatest problems which the early Christian preachers encountered was the question why, if Jesus Christ was really the promised Messiah, his own people Israel did not accept him. One popular response from the Christian preachers was to claim that during the days of his earthly ministry Jesus did not intend any but the intimate group of disciples to accept him (Mark 4.11), and even they only came to realize the truth gradually (Mark 7.18; 8.33; 9.32). It was therefore argued that Jesus not only did not seek publicity, but actually told the people whom he healed to keep quiet about it. A striking example of the introduction of this idea may be found in Matt. 9.30, where Jesus tells the two blind men whose sight he has restored to make sure that no one knows about it. The unreasonable and even absurd nature of this instruction is obvious. How could the blind men prevent people from knowing about it? They could have no control over people knowing about their sight, yet we notice that Jesus did not tell them not to tell anyone. He told them to ensure that nobody knew. So anxious was Mark to introduce his theory about why people did not believe in Jesus during his lifetime that he introduced the idea regardless of whether it made sense or not.

Another way of explaining why the Jewish people during the time of Jesus did not respond to him in greater numbers was suggested by the passage from Isaiah 6. The Jewish people were afflicted with disbelief; their minds and their understanding were clouded so that they could not recognize Jesus. In this context, the idea that the people had closed their eyes suggested itself, and Isaiah 6.10 provided the stimulus. So Matthew, commenting upon the failure of his hearers to understand the words of Jesus, says quite explicitly:

'With them indeed is fulfilled the prophecy of Isaiah that says "You will indeed listen, but never understand, and you will indeed look, but never perceive. For this people's heart has grown dull, and their ears are hard of hearing, and they have shut their eyes; so that they might not look with their eyes, and listen with their ears, and understand with their heart and turn – and I would heal them".' (Matt. 13.14f).

The idea that only the disciples were meant to understand Jesus is referred to in Luke 8.10, where Jesus says to them, 'To you it has been given to know the secrets of the kingdom of God; but to others I speak in parables, so that "looking they may not perceive, and listening they may not understand".' Mark seems to suggest that there was something predestined about the failure of the people to understand Jesus and, like Luke, he hints at the idea that the parables were actually intended to prevent the people from understanding. Only the inner ring of faithful followers were meant to recognize Jesus, and he spoke to them privately about the inner meaning of the parables because the kingdom of God was a secret. The disciples were privileged to know the secret, but the mass of the people had to hear it in parables, 'that they may indeed look, but not perceive, and may indeed listen, but not understand' (Mark 4.13). Even the disciples took some time to understand about Jesus and his message, and on several occasions Jesus rebukes them for their failure to grasp his meaning and uses the metaphor of blindness. When they are in a boat crossing the lake, just after the feeding of the five thousand, the disciples are worried because they have not brought any bread with them. Jesus says to them 'Why are you talking about having no bread? Do you still not perceive or understand? Are your hearts hardened? Do you have eyes, and fail to see? Do you have ears, and fail to hear? And do you not remember?' (Mark 8.17–18).

The Fourth Gospel makes use of the same idea. The contemporaries of Jesus 'could not believe, because Isaiah also said, "He has blinded their eyes, and hardened their heart, so that they might not look with their eyes, and understand with their heart and turn – and I would heal them"' (John 12.40). Once again, we notice the influence of the passage from Isaiah 6, which is thus found in all four of the Gospels. It is against this background that we must interpret the healing of the blind people in the Gospels. They are not just miracles; they are parables of coming to faith in Jesus. In particular, the miracle of the blind man in Mark 8.22–26, who first became partially sighted and then saw clearly, is not just a miracle which shows how Jesus had to make use of the healing gestures twice before a cure could be affected, but is a parable of the way in which the disciples came to have gradual understanding.[13]

However, before the Gospels were written, the metaphor of blindness was already well established in the Christian churches. Paul, for example speaks of the Jewish teachers in the following way: 'and if you are sure that you are a guide to the blind, a light to those who are in darkness, a corrector of the foolish, a teacher of children, having in the law the embodiment of knowledge and truth . . .' (Rom. 2.19f.). Here we see that blindness is the same as darkness, foolishness and childish ignorance. Those who had adopted the Christian way could be described as having 'the eyes of your heart enlightened' (Eph. 1.18). Similarly, if Christians do not live a consistent Christian life, it may be said of them that 'whoever lacks these things is nearsighted and blind, and is forgetful of the cleansing of past sins' (II Peter 1.9). It is characteristic of the metaphor of blindness as used in the Bible that the positive elements of blindness and its popular charisma are overlooked. Blind people are often credited with having highly retentive memories, but in the passage just quoted the apostle equates blindness with forgetfulness.

Blindness as a joke

> The King and his men marched to Jerusalem against the
> Jebusites, the inhabitants of the land, who said to David,
> 'You will not come in here, even the blind and the lame will
> turn you back' – thinking, 'David cannot come in here' . . .
> David had said on that day, 'Whoever would strike down
> the Jebusites, let him get up the water shaft to attack the
> lame and the blind, those whom David hates.' Therefore it
> is said, 'The blind and the lame shall not come into the
> house.' (II Sam. 5.6, 8).

When David, who was king in Hebron, decided to attack
Jerusalem, the defenders of the city mocked him by saying,
'Even if our city was defended by disabled people, you are so
puny that you would not be able to capture it.' It seemed,
however, that David had a more intimate knowledge of
the city than the Jebusites gave him credit for, because he
knew the layout of the water conduits. Responding to the
mockery with his own humour, David said to his men, 'Well,
I can't bear disabled people, so since the city is defended by
blind and lame people, let us be cunning and attack them by
going up the water shafts.' So David captured the city and
made it his new capital. This is the origin, so the story goes,
of the common saying 'The blind and the lame shall not come
into the house'.

This is an odd and rather unpleasant little story. I have an
old jazz recording from the 1930s, and between the tracks you
can sometimes hear the members of the band calling to one
another. At one point somebody calls out, 'You're so dumb
you oughta be the president of the deaf and dumb society'.
This sort of good-natured humour at the expense of disabled
people would be considered in poor taste today. Indeed, if a
child in a classroom shouted out something like that to a class-
mate, there would be a speedy rebuff from the teacher. The
Jebusites, however, were made of tougher stuff and you can

almost hear the soldiers defending the wall roaring with laughter at their captain's joke. Whether there were any real blind and lame people in the city we do not know, but if so, they stayed well hidden, knowing that at such a time it was perfectly true that they were not very useful to the community. The same is true of children and old people, but if the Jebusites had shouted out, 'You wouldn't be able to get in even if children were defending the walls', it would not have been such a good joke.

David's reply has a rather grim note. It is comic, of course, in that the original joke is mocked but when David said that his soul hated blind and lame people, possibly there was more truth in this than he knew. After all, the grandson of the former king, Saul, and a possible claimant to the throne, had been lame in both feet ever since an accident in his childhood (II Sam. 4.4). When David had an opportunity to consider the implications of this, he made sure that he always knew exactly what Mephibosheth was up to (II Sam. 9.1–7). His caution was justified, for at the time of the great rebellion Mephibosheth thought it might be his opportunity to get the throne back (II Sam 16.1–4) and even on the day of the king's triumph, Mephibosheth was still causing the king trouble and pleading his lameness as an excuse for his failure to provide support (II Sam. 19.26). So David had some reason, at least later in his life, to be suspicious of lame people, and although Mephibosheth was still a child when the accident injured him, no doubt David knew about it and had his own thoughts. There is no record that David ever had any problems with blind people, but in spite of the outstanding sensitivity to justice and mercy which he sometimes showed, he no doubt shared in the general prejudice of his age.

It is curious that the proverb does not really fit the story which is supposed to account for its origin. The proverb says that the blind and lame would not go into the house, but the story is about blind and lame people preventing others from coming into the city. It seems likely that the proverb really has its origin in the prohibition against disabled people becoming priests in the temple (Lev. 21.16–23).

The blindness of the sighted: Elisha and the soldiers

The King of Aram sends his armies to arrest Elisha, whose servant is alarmed when he sees the Aramean army encamped around them. But Elisha says to him, 'Do not be afraid, for there are more with us than there are with them'. Then Elisha prays: 'O Lord, please open his eyes that he may see'. So the Lord opens the eyes of the servant, and he sees: that the mountain is full of horses and chariots of fire all around Elisha. When the Arameans come down against him, Elisha prays to the Lord, and says, 'Strike this people, please, with blindness'. So he strikes them with blindness as Elisha had asked (II Kings 6.16–18).

At this stage of the story we have a paradox. The faithful but unseeing sighted one is taught to see, but the unfaithful seeing ones lose the capacity to see at all. The story continues.

Elisha says to them, 'This is not the way, and this is not the city; follow me, and I will bring you to the man whom you seek'. He leads them to Samaria (II Kings 6.19).

As soon as they enter Samaria, Elisha says, 'O Lord, open the eyes of these men that they may see' (vv. 19–20). The words of Elisha in this prayer are almost the same as the words uttered when he asks that the young man's eyes should be opened. The prayer of Elisha has the power to switch sight on and off at will.

The Lord opens their eyes, and they see that they are inside Samaria. When the king of Israel sees them he says to Elisha, 'Father, shall I kill them? Shall I kill them?' He answers, 'No! Did you capture with your sword and your bow those whom you want to kill? Set food and water before them so that they may eat and drink; and let them go to their master.' So he prepares a great feast for them, after they have eaten and drunk, he sends them on their way (vv. 20–22).

We have here two stories involving people who lack perception but their sight is restored. In the first case, that of the young man who is Elisha's servant, we have the story of a faithful person who lacks faith but is given a deeper realization of the truth. In the other case, that of the Aramean soldiers, we find unfaithful people who first lose their perception altogether and then have it restored. Thus, there is a parallel between sight and insight on the one hand, and blindness and sight on the other hand. Blindness is to sight as sight is to insight.

The Song of Hannah

The stories of Hannah, her son Samuel and the priest Eli are rich in auditory and non-visual imagery, and we see this first in Hannah's song of praise to God after she had kept her promise of giving Samuel to Eli for service in the house of the Lord in Shiloh (I Sam. 2.2–10).

There is an emphasis in this song upon speaking. In verse 1 the singer says, 'My mouth derides my enemies, because I rejoice in my victory', and the proud and arrogant are told, 'Talk no more so very proudly, let not arrogance come from your mouth' (v. 3). When God speaks, God 'will thunder in heaven' (v. 10), and this emphasis upon speaking or shouting loudly is in striking contrast to the almost inaudible nature of Hannah's prayer in the temple when she was asking for a child (I Sam. 1.13). It is noticeable how solid are the images in this psalm. 'There is no rock like our God' (I Sam 2.2). The needy are lifted 'from the ash-heap' (v. 8), which is a particularly tactile image. So many of the things mentioned in the psalm invoke tactile images for blind people. The poor are made to 'sit with princes and inherit a seat of honour' (v. 8).

The memory of having sat in a particular chair is often the main impression blind people bring away with them from a meeting, or a visit to a stately home or a cathedral. Many times I have wondered at the massive bishop's throne in a cathedral, or admired the carved legs and the lofty back of a beautiful chair. Another memory I bring away from stately homes and cathedrals is of the pillars. Sighted people generally walk past such things, but blind people like to lean against them, to make contact with the shape and texture of the pillar and imagine what must be up there, if it takes this kind of massive pillar to support it. 'For the pillars of the earth are the Lord's, and on them he has set the world' (v. 8).

Even when warfare is referred to, the particular weapon that is mentioned is the bow, surely one of the most beautiful objects, as one feels the powerful curvature of the wood and the massive strength and tightness of the bowstring. A similar observation could be made about the scales (v. 3), always an interesting object for a blind person to feel. Not only are the weights themselves satisfying to hold, but the beautiful balance of the two sides is interesting and can be explored without sight. So it is that by God 'actions are weighed'.

It is characteristic of the blind condition that there are many things one wants to know and has difficulty in finding out. It is consistent with this that Hannah describes God as 'A God of knowledge' (v. 3). We notice also the emphasis in the psalm upon inwardness, emotions and bodily experiences, which to blind people are so vivid and real. 'My heart exults' and 'my strength is exalted' and I am strongly aware of 'my mouth' (v. 1); 'the feeble gird on strength' – you think of the sensation of lifting up a heavy weapon – and you are aware that your stomach is either full of bread or empty (v. 5a) and are power-fully aware of the birthing experience (v. 5b).

Many disabled people are deeply conscious of their infirmity, and also of the thought that God is the giver of strength and weakness. Moreover, God is on the side of the disabled and the infirm (vv. 6–8). 'He raises up the poor from the dust' (v. 8).

A blind person who reads the psalm in this way will respond particularly to v. 9: 'He will guard the feet of his faithful ones, but the wicked shall be cut off in darkness'. As long as my feet are guarded I do not feel that I am in darkness, but when I am lost and alone, then I am conscious again of being in the dark.

These characteristics are not uncommon in the book of Psalms, and this is not surprising, considering that many of them are prayers based on the analogy between praying and speaking, listening and being heard, and many of the psalms are explicitly dedicated to particular musical instruments. Reading through the psalms from the blind person's point of view, it is not until Psalm 8.3 that we come to something which is distinctly and uniquely visual: 'When I look at your heavens, the work of your fingers, the moon and the stars that you have established'. Before then, we find walking, standing and sitting (Ps. 1.1); a fruit tree planted beside water (1.3); chaff being driven along before the wind (1.4); the breaking of bonds and laughter (2.3, 4); smashing pots to bits with an iron rod (2.9); kissing someone's feet (2.12); having a shield (3.3); hearing someone shouting at you from a hilltop (3.4); lying down to sleep and waking peacefully (3.5); being surrounded by crowds of people (3.6); being struck on the cheek and having your teeth broken by a blow (3.7); finding room to move in (4.1); keeping silence (4.4); being led and having a straight path before you (5.8); singing (5.11); being ticked off (6.1); having aching bones (6.2); crying and making your pillow wet with tears (6.6); weak eyesight (6.7); being threatened by a lion (7.2); being trampled to the ground (7.5); feeling the sharp edge of a sword (7.12); exploring the shaft of an arrow (7.13); falling into a hole (7.15); being hit on the head (7.16); hearing babies cry and little children sing hymns (8.2); and feeling the strength of a wall (8.2).

In those opening psalms, until we come to the reference to the stars, sun and moon (8.3), the only references to visual experience are the prayer that God would lift up the light of his countenance upon us (4.6), the idea of preparing a sacrifice and keeping watch over it (5.3) and the reference to standing before the eyes of God (5.5). Although the Bible is primarily written by sighted people for sighted people, the Psalms, whether attributed to David or Hannah, are rich in expressions with which blind people can identity.

To heal or to transform through acceptance

Care for the injured and the weak, do not ridicule the lame, protect the maimed, and let the blind have a vision of my splendour. Protect the old and the young within your walls. (II. Esd. 2.21 f.)

They [the idols of the heathen] cannot save anyone from death or rescue the weak from the strong. They cannot restore sight to the blind; they cannot rescue one who is in distress. (The Letter of Jeremiah (Baruch) 6.36f.)

These passages present contrasting theologies of disability. The first, from II Esdras, is a beautiful passage in which the people are called upon to renew their covenant with God in justice, mercy and peace. The community is to be transformed through acceptance and inclusion. Differences between people are not to be greeted with ridicule but to be accepted peacefully. Whereas quite often in the Bible one gets the impression that blind people have somehow failed to meet the standard of a perfect creation and are thus excluded from intimacy with God, in this remarkable passage the religious equality of blind people is affirmed. Without ceasing to be genuinely blind, visually impaired people can nevertheless have a vision of the divine splendour. Blindness is not an impediment in the holy place where God's glory is to be seen.

The passage from the Letter of Jeremiah[14] represents an inferior theology. We are now in the atmosphere of a crude competition between the true and the false gods, and a simple list of criteria is offered to tell the difference. A characteristic of the false gods is that they are unable to restore the sight of blind people. The consequence of this crude theology of intervention is that blind people who remain in their blindness, and may even behold a vision of the divine splendour, are regarded as being under the power of an idol or demon simply because they continue to be blind. It is the survival of this approach to blindness, often reinforced by the healing miracles in the Gospels, which makes some sighted Christians feel uncomfortable in the presence of blind Christians.

In September 1996, when I was lecturing in Seoul, I was invited to speak at a church for disabled people. This was a remarkable experience for me. There were about twenty or twenty-five there. Some were lame or had lost part of a limb. Some were in wheelchairs, others were deaf or had speech defects. Others, like myself, were blind or partially sighted. I asked them why it was necessary for them to have their own special church. 'Oh,' they replied, 'it's because the people in the ordinary churches say that we make them feel uncomfortable.' I spoke to them about the disabled persons' God, and then we held hands (if we had any) and sang until the tears ran down our cheeks. On the way back in the car, my host said, 'Now you have experienced *enyuan*.' This is a Confucian concept and refers to the joyful solidarity which is experienced by the oppressed when they encounter deliverance. 'When the Lord restored the fortunes of Zion, we were like those who dream. Then our mouth was filled with laughter, and our tongue with shouts of joy' (Ps. 126.1f.) It was sad that the people in the ordinary churches, controlled by their rigid view of perfection and their competitive God, could not share in that joy.

Restoring or accepting: Two policies towards blindness

> I will lead the blind by a road they do not know, by paths they have not known I will guide them. I will turn the darkness before them into light, the rough places into level ground. These are the things I will do, and I will not forsake them. (Isa. 42.16)

Restoration of sight is a distinctive feature of the activity of God as Saviour and Redeemer in the Bible. In Psalm 146.8 we read, 'the Lord opens the eyes of the blind, the Lord lifts up those who are bowed down'. This is a particular feature of the coming reign of God. When Isaiah is describing the Messianic age, he says, 'Then the eyes of the blind shall be opened, and the ears of the deaf unstopped; then the lame shall leap like a deer, and the tongue of the speechless sing for joy' (Isa. 35.5f.). This is to be one of the characteristics of the work of the Servant of the Lord, whose mission is described in the famous series of psalms which begin in Isaiah 42.

> I am the Lord, I have called you in righteousness,
>   I have taken you by the hand and kept you;
> I have given you as a covenant to the people,
>   a light to the nations,
>   to open the eyes that are blind,
> to bring out the prisoners from the dungeon,
>   from the prison those who sit in darkness.
>
>   (Isa. 42. 6f.)

It is all the more remarkable, in view of the popularity of the idea that God would open the eyes of the blind, to find that in the passage quoted at the heading of this section, no such thing takes place. Blind people are not changed, restored or miraculously healed. They are accepted and the behaviour of others around them is modified to give them equal opportunities.

To blind people, familiarity is all important. When I am walking on one of my familiar paths, I need no assistance. It is when I venture into the unknown that I become hesitant. The opening up of a new route is as much an adventure as blazing a new trail through the wilderness. It is almost impossible to do this when sighted people are around, because one inevitably gives the impression of being lost. To sighted people, the behaviour of an exploring blind person cannot be distinguished from the behaviour of a lost blind person. When you are lost, you are not exploring the unknown, because you do not know whether the place you are at is known or not. You have become disoriented. When you are exploring a new route, you are oriented towards the direction of the route. However, this necessarily involves exploring perimeters, going around all four corners of a square, tracing the lawn right around the quadrangle in order to find out where it goes. To sighted people watching, the desire to help is irresistible, and very understandable and forgivable. It is self-defeating, however, for when a blind person is being helped it is more difficult for him or her to learn independence on the new route.

In the situation where you do not have to learn a route but simply need to get somewhere, then a guide is important. There is no point in learning the route, since you probably will not come that way again. So we see that the words in Isa. 42.16 are most appropriate, 'I will lead the blind by a road they do not know'. In other words, because they are passing through a strange territory, I will be their guide. There is no need for them to learn the route because they are being led into a new land. Therefore the Lord will lead us in paths which we have not known. It does not mean that God will deliberately lead us into places we do not know; it means that because we do not know the way, God will lead us. By this process of guidance, the darkness in front of us will be turned into light. When I am touching the elbow of an experienced and trusted guide, I do not have to worry about falling into a trench or stumbling down some stairs. It is as if the rough places were turned into level ground – not that rough places present a particular difficulty to blind people, but unexpected ledges and unpredictable rough places are a bit of a problem. God as the guide understands all these techniques. Where would I be now if my guide should suddenly desert me? Would I be able to find my way out, or back? Such questions need not trouble us, because our guide says, 'I will not forsake them'.

Why does God not save all this trouble by simply restoring

our sight? Then God would not have to guide us. Well, it looks as if God likes us the way we are. God enjoys guiding us and likes us to trust God's expert assistance. God does not patronize us but simply gets on with the job, giving us a sense of confidence as we walk. After all, as we allow God to lead us in this way, we are like God's chosen servant. Although sometimes God's servant is described as opening the eyes of the blind, at other times the servant himself is blind. Sometimes this is said ironically, because the servant himself does not seem to understand the high calling of God.

> Listen, you that are deaf;
>   and you that are blind, look up and see!
> Who is blind but my servant,
>   or deaf like my messenger whom I send?
> Who is blind like my dedicated one,
>   or blind like the servant of the Lord?
> He sees many things, but does not observe them;
>   his ears are open, but he does not hear.
>   (Isa. 42.18f.)

The blindness and deafness of the servant, who represents the chosen, suffering people of God, is a metaphor for the failure of the people to interpret their mission, but in Isa. 50.10 the tone is quite different. 'Who among you fears the Lord and obeys the voice of his servant, who walks in darkness and has no light, yet trusts in the name of the Lord and relies upon his God?' In this verse, the model of the blind person who with calm assurance allows God to be the guide is applied to the relationship between God and God's special servant. The trustfulness of the servant who walks calmly forward in the darkness, depending upon God, is a challenge to all who witness it. It is not so much that they look but do not perceive; it is a question of whether they have sufficient faith to follow the example of blind people. Far from having their sight miraculously restored, blind people become a model of faithfulness in their very blindness. A similar ideal is offered by Jeremiah, when he is describing the return of the exiled people to their promised homeland:

> See, I am going to bring them from the land of the north,
>   and gather them from the farthest parts of the earth,
> among them the blind and the lame,
>   those with child and those in labour, together;
>   a great company, they shall return here.
> With weeping they shall come,
>   and with consolations I will lead them back.
>
> (Jer. 31.8f.)

The wonderful thing about this passage is that it does not entice or insult disabled people by amazing promises. It simply says that they will be included along with everyone else in the joyful repatriation. Indeed, they will have as natural a part in the crowd as expectant mothers, for pregnancy is not a disease or a deficiency. Moreover, no matter how great the crisis into which their disability plunges them, they, like the women who are actually in childbirth, will be accepted and assisted in their crisis, and normalized within the community.

An even more dramatic thought is found in Micah, who suggests that disabled people will not only be included in the community of the returning exiles; they will be the very heart and soul of that community.

> In that day, says the Lord,
>   I will assemble the lame
> and gather those who have been driven away,
>   and those whom I have afflicted.
> The lame I will make the remnant,
>   and those who were cast off, a strong nation;
> and the Lord will reign over them in Mount Zion
>   now and for evermore.
>
> (Mic. 4.6f.)

To some extent, the idea is that there is no limit to God's restoring power. Perhaps the able-bodied people were a bit bothered about the long return journey, but Micah says that even if they were disabled, God would bring them back. Indeed, God prefers the lame and other people who in weakness and disability have been driven out, because in a very special way they symbolize the alienated and oppressed people whom God delights to deliver. We notice also that they are delivered not by being saved from their disabilities, in a series of healing miracles, but by becoming the people of God. Their delight is not in ceasing to be disabled but in having God as their Redeemer and King.

Now we can return to the passages where the restoration of sight is promised. It is important to realize that this is not offered as a wonderful miracle, of the kind that would startle the medical profession, as is claimed in so many modern healing crusades. Rather, it is almost always in the context of the restoration of an oppression, the setting right of an injustice. We referred to Psalm 146, where it says that the Lord opens the eyes of the blind and lifts up those who are bowed down. It is time now to consider the context of these promises. In verse 7, God it described as one who 'executes justice for the oppressed; who gives food to the hungry. The Lord sets the prisoners free', and then we have (v. 8), 'The Lord opens the eyes of the blind'. This is the first place (not necessarily the oldest) in the Bible where opening of the eyes of the blind is mentioned, and we fail to understand this unless we recognize that it is in the context not of a medical miracle but of the determination of God to rectify injustice. Those who remove miracles of healing from this justice context are not faithful to the spirit of scripture. Too often, they literalize the illustration and forget the context. Their hearts are set on the sensationalism of the miracle rather than on the social and political calling to alleviate the oppressed.

Vanishing and knowing/knowing and vanishing

And the angel of the Lord vanished from his sight. Then Gideon perceived that it was the angel of the Lord; and Gideon said 'Help me, Lord God! For now I have seen the angel of the Lord face to face.' (Judg. 6.21–22)

Then their eyes were opened, and they recognized him; and he vanished from their sight. They said to each other, 'Were not our hearts burning within us while he was talking to us on the road?' (Luke 24.31–32)

Gideon is working in the barn on his father's farm when the angel of the Lord appears to him, calling him to take up arms against the Midianite oppressor. Gideon is fairly sure that his visitor is a divine messenger, or even the living God, but he needs confirmation. 'Show me a sign that it is you who speak with me' (Judg. 6.17). Gideon asks the angel to remain until he has made ready some presents, and the angel agrees. Gideon then prepares a meal and brings it out and places it on a rock for the visitor. When the angel touches the food with the tip of his staff, fire comes from the rock and burns up the offering. At that moment, the angel vanishes and Gideon perceives that it was the angel of the Lord (v. 18).

The story of the birth of Samson is rather similar. Manoah and his wife (we are not told her name) are informed by an angel that they are to have a son. It is not quite so clear in this case that they did recognize the messenger as being divine, because they spoke of him as a man of God, and the text specifically says 'Manoah did not know that he was the angel of the Lord' (Judg. 13.16). Manoah asks the messenger his name, but the angel refuses to disclose it. However, the couple have been told that they could offer to God a burnt sacrifice. This is prepared, laid upon a rock and used as an altar.

When the flame went up toward heaven from the altar, the angel of the Lord ascended in the flame of the altar while Manoah and his wife looked on; and they fell on their faces to the ground. The angel of the Lord did not appear again to Manoah and his wife. Then Manoah realized that it was the angel of the Lord. (vv. 20–21)

In both these passages the recognition follows the vanishing. It is indeed the manner of vanishing which reveals the identity of the messenger. However, in the New Testament story of the Emmaus road (Luke 24.13–35), the sequence is reversed. Two disciples are walking from Jerusalem on the road to the village of Emmaus. They are talking about the terrible events which had taken place only two days earlier, when Jesus had been crucified. A stranger overtakes them and asks them what they are talking about, but they do not recognize him as the resurrected Christ until he sits down to supper with them. Then he vanishes from their sight. In this story recognition precedes vanishing.

These three stories show the biblical imagery grappling with the limits of the symbolism of sight. Although one may sometimes see God (Isa 6.1; Ezek. 1.1; Rev. 1.7), in general God is unseeable. There is the limit of human sight, and there is the limit of the metaphor of sight when used to describe God. It is as Gideon, and then Manoah and his wife, realize the inability of sight to maintain a fixed gaze, that is, as the divine messenger vanishes, that in the vanishing (in the realization of the limits of sight) they penetrate the mystery. In the case of the Emmaus story, the recognition of the divine visitor is not obtained through experiencing the limits of sight, but through the action of breaking bread. It is after they recognize the risen Christ that he can no longer remain visible, but they recognize him not through the vanishing itself but through the breaking of bread.

If we regard inability to see as the equivalence of blindness, these stories develop various aspects of blindness and sight in relation to religious experience. Gideon and Manoah with his wife are blind although they see. When they fail to see, their eyes are opened. The disciples on the Emmaus road see the stranger, but 'Their eyes were kept from recognizing him' (Luke 24.16). When the stranger breaks bread, their eyes are opened, but at the moment of their vision they become blind again as far as he is concerned, for he vanishes from their sight.

So we see that in the Bible knowledge is not always equated with sight. There can be unseeing sight, and recognition of that which is no longer seen. Moreover, the Emmaus story tells us that there are two ways of not seeing. While the stranger walks with them along the road, they are blind in ignorance and unbelief; they cannot recognize him. When the stranger takes the bread and breaks it, their eyes are opened but immediately this is followed by a second kind of blindness, the blindness of recognition. We shall consider the meaning of this in the next section.

The blindness of despair and the blindness of hope: The road to Emmaus

> While they were talking and discussing, Jesus himself came near and went with them, but their eyes were kept from recognizing him. (Luke 24.15f.)

As the two disciples were walking along the road from Jerusalem to Emmaus their hearts grieved over the things which had happened in Jerusalem. Jesus had been crucified, and that very morning, some women of their company had amazed them by reporting that they had seen him alive. While they are talking and wondering about what all this could mean, Jesus himself draws near and walks with them, but their eyes are kept from recognizing him. It is as if they are blind. A stranger is there, they hear his voice, they converse with him, yet they are unable to recognize him.

Often it is like that in blindness. Someone comes along but

does not introduce himself. You walk together and talk. There
is a vague familiarity about the voice. Could it be so-and-so?
But no, that person is far away, or even dead. Somehow you
have left it too late to say outright, 'Who are you?' By now
you should know, but you still do not know.

Soon the village is in sight, and the friends (are they husband
and wife?) come to the door of their house. The stranger seems
to be going on further, but they say to him, 'Stay with us,
because it is almost evening and the day is now nearly over'
(v. 29). As they eat together, the stranger takes the bread,
breaks it and gives it to them. 'Then their eyes were opened,
and they recognized him; and he vanished from their sight'
(v. 31).

The moment their blindness is overcome, they become blind
again, since blindness and invisibility complement each other.
'He vanished out of their sight' means that they could no
longer see him. It is not just that he walks away; their powers
of sight are no longer effective. The limits of perception are
reached. He vanishes, and there they are, once again unable
to see him just as they were unable to recognize him on the
Emmaus road.

The second blindness, however, was vastly different from
the first. When the stranger first met them on the road, their
eyes were kept from recognizing him through their sadness,
their preoccupation with their own loss, and their despair. We
may call this the blindness of loss and doubt. When once again
their eyes became useless after the breaking of the bread, the
blindness which they had with respect to Jesus was full of joy.
Recognition is followed by a second blindness. To see him is
immediately not to see him. Just as St Paul says that in Christ
neither circumcision nor uncircumcision matters, but only a
new person in Christ (Gal. 5.6), so we may conclude of this
Emmaus story that neither blindness nor sight matter, but only
a new hope in Jesus Christ.

The hand and the eye

> The eye cannot say to the hand, 'I have no need of you.'
> (I Cor. 12.21)

Well, I suppose if you are walking around an art gallery, the
eye can indeed say to the hand 'I have no need of you'. Similarly, when you are at the cinema, the theatre, or a football
match, the eye has no need of the hand, although it would be
difficult to clap or eat an ice-cream in the interval. By way of
contrast, there are many cases where the hand does not need
the eye. When you are using the telephone, the hand does not
need the eye in order to key in the number or answer a call, and
the hand is completely independent when you are touch-typing.
There is a whole range of modern computer equipment for
which the hand is sufficient. Although we think the hand
needs the eye for many daily tasks, it probably doesn't. For
example, when you are doing up your shoe-laces, you probably
look at your fingers from habit if you are sighted, but if you
practised looking away in some other direction, you would
soon find that your fingers knew how to tie the knot. Our
fingers know more than we often give them credit for. The
hands do not really need the eyes when you are playing the
piano. Some of the world's greatest pianists are blind and many
sighted pianists close their eyes. You can play chess with your
hands and you do not need your eyes. When you are out
walking, you need either your eyes or your hands, but not
both. With eyes you do not need your hands to manipulate
the long white cane, but without eyes your hands are needed
for this purpose.

There are some activities where at least one hand definitely
needs at least one eye – driving a car, for example. On the
whole, however, it is mouths rather than hands that need
eyes. It is difficult to have a conversation with the mouth
only. It is the eyes that hold the attention of the person to
whom you are speaking. Although what is said may or

may not be of interest, the mouth itself is seldom interesting, except to deaf people and lovers; it is the eyes that hold the attention.

5

Blindness observed

The grief of blindness

Throughout the book of Job there are references to blindness. Generally, these describe somebody blinded by grief rather than somebody grieving over blindness, but the metaphors are so vivid that they convey the dismay and horror of someone who has recently lost sight. 'My face is red with weeping, and deep darkness is on my eyelids' (Job 16.16). 'My eye has grown dim from grief, and all my members are like a shadow' (Job 17.7). This describes very well the experience of a recently blinded person, who feels that his or her legs have more or less disappeared. One can only tell where they are by moving them, or touching them. Sighted people describe their experiences of a deep fog or of being in a cave by saying, 'You couldn't see your hand in front of your face', and when this happens you feel that your hand has become unreal. Your body no longer casts a shadow on a sunny day and you no longer have a reflection in a mirror. So you start to feel that you yourself are a shadow.

'They are thrust from light into darkness, and driven out of the world' (Job 18.18). This experience could be repeated by many people who have suddenly lost their sight. A soldier in the Falklands war told me how he lifted his head above the parapet for a moment and both his eyes were taken out by shrapnel. In that instant, he was thrust from being a normal sighted person to being a totally blind person. He told me, 'There was no more than a second in it.'

'He has walled up my way so that I cannot pass, and he has set darkness upon my paths' (Job 19.8). 'If only I could vanish in darkness, and thick darkness would cover my face!' (Job. 23.17). These verses convey very vividly the sense of claustrophobia which often accompanies blindness. In my own experience, now that I have been totally blind for about fifteen years, I only have this claustrophobic sense when I am panicky through getting lost or being ill. As for one's path being hemmed in by darkness, a recently blinded person experimenting with mobility must often feel this. After a while, handling the white cane becomes like turning on a torch, but that only develops with confidence. This feeling of being hemmed in also comes from being confined to familiar paths. There is indeed a band playing over there, but what lies between here and there? We are in a park, so perhaps there will be a pond, and I must proceed very cautiously. It is in unfamiliar and possibly dangerous places that this feeling is particularly strong, for example, when you are carefully picking your way with the white cane through roadworks. I always find that rather unnerving, especially if I have to cross excavated trenches by walking on planks. Part of the problem is that you have no idea how deep the trench is, but you know that if you cannot touch the bottom with your outstretched cane, it is too deep for comfort.

'Oh, that I were as in the months of old, as in the days when God watched over me; when his lamp shone over my head, and by his light I walked through darkness' (Job 29.2). This is a touching description of longing for a past, sighted life. I had that experience about four years after I became a registered blind person, at a time when I had solved most of the immediate problems caused by blindness and just wanted to go back to normal life. I felt as if I had proved whatever God wanted me to prove, and now that the test was over, I wanted to return to what I still thought of as an ordinary life. Some years later a man who had passed through an experience like my own wrote to me telling me of his recurrent dream of living in a perfectly sighted world. 'Do you think', he asked, 'that one ever escapes from the fantasy of perfect vision?'

In familiar surroundings, when I am occupied with something, I seldom have this feeling, or even remember that I am blind. I am not blind; I am just me. However, sometimes when one of my sons is playing football, or when, on a lovely sunny day at the beach, someone is so inconsiderate as to tell me how beautiful the women are in their topless bathing costumes, I may be filled with a sudden pang. As for standing in front of a great rose window in a cathedral, or visiting the Van Gogh Art Gallery in Amsterdam, I am happy enough to be interested in the perceptions of whoever I am with. We are all different.

Entombed within the body

'Their children come to honour, and they do not know it;
    they are brought low, and it goes unnoticed.
They feel only the pain of their own bodies,
    and mourn only for themselves.'

(Job 14.21f.)

The fourteenth chapter of Job is a powerful statement of human mortality. Babies are born like flowers but they wither; human beings are like a passing shadow (v. 2). Even a tree, when it is cut down and its root is old and withered, may bud again at the scent of water, but human beings die and do not return.

The poet imagines himself locked up in Sheol, the place of the dead. He wishes that God had only imprisoned him for a time and would remember him when his sentence is completed, but as the mountains gradually crumble and the very rocks are worn away, hope is finally extinguished. Finally, the dead are imagined as being locked up not so much in Sheol as within their own bodies. Because they are preoccupied with their own pain, and mourning over their own loss, they fail to notice what is going on in the world of the living. The successes and achievements of their children are unnoticed and their troubles and failures go unobserved.

This could be read as a vivid commentary on certain kinds of disability, or perhaps we should say on certain kinds of reaction to disability. Pain fills the body and occupies the consciousness. It is difficult or impossible to pay attention to other people when you are absorbed with pain. One of the blessings of blindness, if I can put it like that, is that usually it is without pain. However, the state of mourning, the interruption of awareness due to endlessly harping upon a sense of loss, which turns first into a grievance and then into bitterness, can also block us off from other people. It is a feature of many disabilities, certainly of physical and sensory impairments, that one becomes hyper-conscious of the body. Anybody who has broken an arm or leg will know how keenly aware you become of what the body can and cannot do. Perhaps the most common experience of this kind for people in the middle and later years of life is back injuries. That jab of pain as you lift a weight or stoop over reminds you that your body does not like that. The gay abandon with which you threw your body down the stairs when you were a teenager is all gone. Now you come down step by step, being glad at each step that there is one less to go. The feeling of disability, however, is not simply that of fragility or weakness, although I have heard many disabled people say that the disability has made them feel old. Certainly, when you are blind and have to step so carefully, wondering all the time if you will smash into something, it can easily make you feel old. For the person in the wheelchair, the body has become the wheelchair and one no longer has the easy grace of fluent movement which other people, using their legs, appear to have. It is the sensory impairments which, most of all, give this feeling of being entombed within one's body. In the case of hearing impairment, it is difficult to enter into the conversation of those around you and you tend, I am told, to lapse into your own thoughts. In the case of visual handicap, the loss of external visual reality can easily lead to a sharp sense of the interior life. Moreover, because you have lost the subtlety of emotion in the faces of the people around you, you can easily fail to realize what is going on. You cannot read the expression of your friend or loved one whilst they are reading a letter; you have to wait until they utter an exclamation (but was it of pain or joy?) or tell you. So much humour is facial – exchanging funny looks, mocking expressions and so on – that it is easy for a blind person to feel left out or to lose interest. This is why music, walking out on a windy day, or the intimacies of sexual love are so important in the lives of many blind people. You are summoned out of yourself to meet reality.

The suffering of blind people

> Blindly they wandered through the streets,
>   so defiled with blood
> that no one was able
>   to touch their garments.
> 'Away! Unclean!' people shouted at them;
>   'Away! Away! Do not touch!'
> So they became fugitives and wanderers.
>   (Lam. 4.14f.)

This passage offers a terrible description of those who wander around blind at the time when Jerusalem is sacked by the Babylonians. Whether the people referred to are blind anyway, or whether they have been blinded or dazed in the fighting, we do not know, nor whether the blood which soaks their clothes is from their own wounds, or whether, in their blindness, they are stumbling around the city falling over the bleeding corpses of the slain. They present a pitiable spectacle but they meet with little pity. Instead of being helped, having their wounds washed and their clothes changed, they become objects of fear and scorn. Treated as untouchables, they have little prospect but death.

This is a situation of terrible crisis, but the situation of most blind people in ancient Israel could not have been very admirable at the best of times. The fact that blindness is generally regarded as the result of a curse from God is illustrated by the threatening words in Deut. 28.28f.:

The Lord will afflict you with madness, blindness, and confusion of mind; you shall grope about at noon as the blind people grope in darkness, but you shall be unable to find your way; and you shall be continually abused and robbed, without anyone to help.

This is probably a pretty accurate picture of the lives of many blind people. There must have been at least a few people who thought it was a bit of a joke to put a stumbling block in the path of a blind person, stand quietly to one side and see what happened, otherwise it would not have been necessary to have a specific law against this (Lev. 19.14), and from the way the prohibition is worded, it is clear that only the very fear of God would prevent this cruel entertainment. Blind people are regarded as being imperfect, and it is agreed that this imperfection is a sort of insult to God. This is why blind people, along with other disabled groups, are not permitted to be priests or to come before the altar in the temple (Lev. 21.18). Similarly, there must have been people who thought it was fun to take a blind person in the opposite direction from where he or she wanted to go and then leave them stranded, because such actions are strictly forbidden (Deut. 27.18). Maybe that was why the old priest Eli, now almost blind, was no longer serving beside the altar (I Sam. 3.2). Perhaps his blindness is mentioned at this point in order to explain how it comes about that the young Samuel is keeping watch over the sanctuary, and not Eli himself. Whether he was forbidden to minister because of his blindness, but was allowed to remain as a sort of caretaker, or whether his blindness made it difficult to tell when the sanctuary lamp was burning or not, we do not know. It must

have been terrible for the old man, gradually losing his sight
and knowing that if it got any worse, and if people knew about
it, he would fall under the prohibitions against disabled priests
and have his ministry taken from him.

The description of the solitary blind person in Job 12.24f.
is probably typical. The verses describe the majesty of God,
but use the figure of a blind person to make the point: 'He . . .
makes them wander in a pathless waste. They grope in the
dark without light; he makes them stagger like a drunkard.'
How easy it is to lose your balance when you are unaccompan-
ied on an unfamiliar road.

Another vivid description of what blind people look like to
their sighted fellow-citizens is found in Isaiah 59. As so often
in such passages, it is a description of a punishment from God
upon the people as a whole:

> Therefore justice is far from us,
>   and righteousness does not reach us;
> we wait for light, and lo! there is darkness;
>   and for brightness, but we walk in gloom.
> We grope like the blind along a wall,
>   groping like those who have no eyes;
> we stumble at noon as in the twilight,
>   among the vigorous as though we were dead . . .
>   (Isa. 59.9–10)

6

Blind Bible/blind God

Beyond light and darkness: Divine and human points of view

> My frame was not hidden from you,
> when I was being made in secret,
>   intricately woven in the depths of the earth.
> Your eyes beheld my unformed substance.
>
> (Ps. 139.15–16)

> Do you have eyes of flesh? Do you see as humans see?
> (Job 10.4)

It is characteristic of the link between sight and knowledge that the eyes should become a symbol of cognition. People may react to this in different ways. God's knowledge may be regarded as sublime, calling forth feelings of amazement. 'I praise thee, for thou art fearful and wonderful! Wonderful are thy works; thou knowest me right well' (Ps. 139.14, RSV). On the other hand, God's knowledge can be thought of as an intrusion, a violation of one's privacy, a peering into one's secrets in a way that arouses contempt. 'Will you not look away . . . until I swallow my spittle?' (Job 7.19).

The contrast between the all-encompassing knowledge of God and the ignorance and helplessness of the human being is expressed most poignantly in the contrast between the innocent life of the foetus being wonderfully fashioned in the womb, and the all-competent, penetrating, yet compassionate gaze of God.

> My frame was not hidden from you,
> when I was being made in secret,
>   intricately woven in the depths of the earth.
> Your eyes beheld my unformed substance.
> In your book were written
>   all the days that were formed for me,
>   when none of them as yet existed.
> How weighty to me are your thoughts, O God!
>   How vast is the sum of them!
> I try to count them – they are more than the sand;
>   I come to the end – I am still with you.
>   (Ps. 139.15–18)

The number of God's thoughts seems to correspond to the intricacy of the cells of the human body. When at last consciousness is brought to life, one is still in the presence of that absolutely loving knowledge.

On the other hand, one can feel pursued, hunted down by this knowledge.

> Your hands fashioned and made me;
>   and now you turn and destroy me.
> Remember that you fashioned me like clay;
>   and will you turn me to dust again?
> Did you not pour me out like milk
>   and curdle me like cheese?
> You clothed me with skin and flesh,
>   and knit me together with bones and sinews.
> You have granted me life and steadfast love,
>   and your care has preserved my spirit.
> Yet these things you hid in your heart;
>   I know that this was your purpose.
>   (Job 10.8–13)

Although God seems to make us and preserve us in love, all the time his purpose is to spy on us, to use his detailed knowledge of us against us, so that he will know exactly where and how we sin.

When we try to defend ourselves by knowing God, it is futile. 'Look, he passes by me, and I do not see him; he moves on, but I do not perceive him' (Job 9.11). Is God invisible, or is it we who are blind? The invisibility of the other and one's own blindness are but two sides of the coin. It is as if there is a one-way mirror between ourselves and God. From our side, we see only the mirror-image of ourselves, our own knowledge cast back upon ourselves. From the other side, God sees every detail of our action, every expression on our faces, although remaining impenetrable. We become vaguely aware that we are observed, even sharply aware; we look around to see who is watching, but there is nothing, only the mirror.

'Can you find out the deep things of God? Can you find out the limit of the Almighty? It is higher than heaven – what can you do? Deeper than Sheol – what can you know?' (Job 11.7f.). Suddenly, however, the frustration of the enigma turns into a sublime sense of presence.

> Such knowledge is too wonderful for me;
>   it is so high that I cannot attain it.
> Where can I go from your spirit?
>   Or where can I flee from your presence?
> If I ascend to heaven, you are there;
>   if I make my bed in Sheol, you are there.
> If I take the wings of the morning
>   and settle at the farthest limits of the sea,
> even there your hand shall lead me,
>   and your right hand shall hold me fast.
>
> (Ps. 139.6–10)

Are you remorselessly pursued by a knowledge which, like a guided missile, tracks you down no matter how much you twist and turn, or are you always in the presence of one who accompanies you into the extremities of your life, the heights and depths of your experience? it is a matter of perspective.

We take a further step into this paradox of perspective if we consider the impact of God's wonderful knowledge upon our mobility.

> O Lord, you have searched me and known me. You know when I sit down and when I rise up; you discern my thoughts from far away. You search out my path and my lying down, and are acquainted with all my ways. Even before a word is on my tongue, O Lord, you know it completely. You hem me in, behind and before, and lay your hand upon me. (Ps. 139.1–5)

Here we have a picture of an all-encompassing knowledge which protects and guides and which is intimate rather than intrusive. One is aware of the joyful wonder of being known, like the child who gets on the roundabout and cries out 'Look daddy! Look at me!' There is a moment of anxiety as the great machine begins to turn. Mum and Dad are no longer to be seen. Then around you go, and there they are! The parents wave and shout, and the child grins with delight and waves back, and then is whirled away. There is something so exciting and so comforting about this rhythm of absence and presence – a pleasure of absence, the threat of which is acceptable because of the assurance of reunion.

On the other hand, the same experience can be interpreted as a constraint. He 'makes them wander in a pathless waste. They grope in the dark without light; he makes them stagger like a drunkard' (Job. 12.24f.).

> If I go forward, he is not there; or backward, I cannot perceive him; on the left he hides, and I cannot behold him; I turn to the right, but I cannot see him. But he knows the way that I take ... My foot has held fast to his steps. (Job 23.8–11)

It is as if you are playing hide-and-seek with God, who is like a will-o'-the-wisp – God is here! No, God is there! – all you know for sure is that God is somewhere. You know that you are following in God's tracks, but so good is God's woodcraft that in the depths of the forest you can never catch a glimpse of God. You may cry out, 'Does not he see my ways, and number all my steps?' (Job 31.4). There is a striking contrast between the one whose steps are all numbered by a dark mystery which remains obscure, and the infinite wonder of the person who exclaims, 'How weighty to me are your thoughts, O God! How vast is the sum of them! I try to count them – they are more than the sand' (Ps. 139.17f.). The one person fears that his or her steps are numbered; the other person wonders at the infinite number of the thoughts of God.

It is when we turn to the contrast between darkness and light that the difference between the two perspectives becomes most striking. To speak strictly, it is not so much a contrast between dark and light but a contrast between two ways of experiencing the fact that there is no longer a contrast between darkness and light. One experience says,

> before I go, never to return, to the land of gloom and deep darkness, a land of gloom and chaos, where light is like darkness. (Job 10.21).

> They make night into day; 'The light,' the say, 'is near to the darkness.' If I look for Sheol as my house, if I spread my couch in darkness, if I say to the Pit, 'You are my father', and to the worm, 'My mother', or 'My sister', where then is my hope? Who will see my hope? Will it go down to the bars of Sheol? Shall we descend together into the dust? (Job 17.12–16f)

When one is beyond light and darkness, it can be an experience of terrible confusion. Everything is chaos. Consciousness and unconsciousness become indistinguishable. Nothing is fixed.

The distinction between the conscious and unconscious life becomes vague. On the other hand, if the fact that we are beyond light and darkness is seen from a divine perspective, from the point of view of faith in God, then we see that this characteristic marks the blind person as being uniquely in the image of God. No sighted person can claim to be beyond light and darkness. In so far as this is a characteristic of God, to whom darkness and light are both alike, then the blind person who shares that characteristic is already in the likeness of God. One does not have to be miraculously healed in order to manifest the glory of God (John 9.3). Without blind people, the religious experience of sighted people is not complete.

The struggles of Job in his illness and the sublime meditation of Psalm 139 represent two ways of looking at blindness. Each is the inversion of the other. Even blind people who have faith in God will oscillate between one perspective and the other. The relationship between the two perspectives is like that between the duck and the rabbit in the optical puzzle, when it could be the outline of one or the other, depending on how it strikes you. It is a matter of presuppositions, of a certain readiness for one perspective. Just as, with the duck and the rabbit, it is difficult to hold one perspective firmly, so it is with the human and the divine perspectives on blindness. It swings with one's mood, the happenings of the day, one's dreams and hopes, and many other factors which are unknown and unnameable. Happy is that blind person, however, where the similarity of light and darkness has become a chaos, whose human point of view is challenged, qualified and sometimes briefly replaced by the other point of view; in the state of being beyond light and darkness, one is brought into a strange intimacy with the divine.

God is blind

The Lord has said that he would reside in thick darkness.
(II Chron. 6.1)

In view of the fact that the Bible comes from a sighted world
and is addressed to a sighted world in which sight stands for
knowledge and power while blindness stands for ignorance
and weakness, it is not surprising that nowhere in the Bible is
God said to be blind, although there are many places where
God is said to be sighted. However, human sight is defective,
whereas God's knowledge is perfect. Therefore sight was never
regarded as an entirely adequate way of describing God. This
led to various ways of qualifying the idea that God has sight,
including the belief that God's vision penetrates to the interior,
whereas human vision remains with outward appearances
(I Sam. 16.7), and that God is one who sees in secret
(Matt. 5.4).

This idea of the limits of sight is extended in expressions
which speak of God as being beyond sight or not needing
sight. The outstanding example of this is Ps. 139.12, where
the Psalmist says that darkness and light are both alike to God.

Another way of indicating that God is beyond sight, or that
his nature transcends the character of human sight, is to
describe God as being wrapped in thick darkness. This is, to
all intents and purposes, to be blind. A human being wrapped
in deep darkness would be virtually blind or temporarily
experiencing the state of blindness, and so we may say that all
the places where God is described in this way can be appropri-
ated by blind people.

'He made darkness his covering around him, his canopy
thick clouds dark with water' (Ps. 18.11). The Psalmist is
describing God as the thunder God, the God of the storm
clouds, but the King James Bible (the Authorized Version) has
a beautiful expression: 'He made darkness his hiding place'. A
few verses before, God is described as descending with 'thick

darkness ... under his feet' (v. 9). Blind people are used to having thick darkness under their feet, and so God participates in our experience.

'The Lord is king! Let the earth rejoice; let the many coastlands be glad! Clouds and thick darkness are all around him; righteousness and justice are the foundation of his throne' (Ps. 97.1–2). This not only suggests that human sight cannot penetrate the darkness that surrounds God, but also that God is indifferent to this darkness. God is used to it. It makes no difference to God.

In the book of Job there is a fine description of God as one who is familiar with the darkness: 'He uncovers the deeps out of darkness, and brings deep darkness to light' (Job 12.22). Once again, the AV is more beautiful and meaningful for blind people: 'He discovereth deep things out of darkness'. This does not exactly mean that God brings the dark things to light, but that in the darkness he discovers deep things. All blind people know that in the darkness there are indeed deep things, but they are not unknown to God nor are they foreign to God's nature.

Not only is God at home in the darkness and, we might say, indifferent to it, able to bring out of darkness its deep mysteries, but God is also the giver of darkness. God is not only a giver of light, but also of darkness. It is God's gift. 'You make darkness, and it is night' (Ps. 104.20); 'I form the light and create darkness' (Isa. 45.7). It is because the darkness belongs to God that God can say, 'I will give you the treasures of darkness' (Isa. 45.3). These passages are sufficient to show us that in the Kingdom of God not only are there neither male nor female, slaves and free (Gal. 3.28), but there are also neither blind nor sighted. There is a God of blind people and there is a God of sighted people, but beyond and above there is the God above the gods, who transcends both blindness and sight and is the God of everyone.

Elijah and the angel: the beauty of being touched

> Then he lay down under the broom tree and fell asleep. Suddenly an angel touched him and said to him, 'Get up and eat.' He looked, and there at his head was a cake baked on hot stones, and a jar of water. He ate and drank, and lay down again. The angel of the Lord came a second time, touched him, and said, 'Get up and eat, otherwise the journey will be too much for you.' (I Kings 19.5–7)

Queen Jezebel had vowed to kill Elijah and he was running to save his life. Exhausted, he had to rest. He fell asleep, and what followed is a strange mixture of reality and dreaming. If it is a dream, it is a double dream, of the sort which is not unknown elsewhere in the Bible. Pharaoh, for example, had a double dream, first of fat cows and thin cows coming out of the river, and next of ripe sheaves of wheat consumed by thin and diseased wheat. Earlier in his life, Joseph himself had a double dream in which first the sheaves of barley bowed down to his sheaf and then the sun, moon and stars bowed down to him as well, but there is no other case in the Bible of a tactile dream.

You sometimes hear about people who dream that they are floating in a warm sea, only to wake up and find that the hot water bottle has burst; or that they are in a collision, only to wake up suddenly and find that they have fallen out of bed. These might be described as tactile dreams, or at least dreams with a kinaesthetic quality. Of course, the dreams of blind people often have tactile or kinaesthetic qualities such as being jostled in a crowd, and dreams of eating are quite common. In such cases, we are reminded of the theory of Sigmund Freud, that the dream is sometimes intended to protect our sleep by providing us with an imagined gratification. So the hungry person who still needs sleep dreams of eating instead of being woken up by hunger.

The case of Elijah's double dream is more unusual. The

touch of the angel, if it was in a dream, was meant to wake him up, unless we assume that the whole thing was a dream repeated in two parts. In that case, Elijah only ate in his dream, and it was the power of the dream that kept him running for forty days and forty nights.

On the other hand, perhaps none of this was a dream. Perhaps he was really touched by an angel and woke to find real food waiting for him, nice and hot as well. The angel woke him again, like a mother insisting that her children eat up, and made him have some more.

There is at least one other case where a human being was touched by an angel: Jacob at the Brook Jabbok. Jacob actually wrestled with the angel all night, and in the end the angel touched him and dislocated his thigh (Gen. 32.24–31). In Gen. 6.4 we read that the sons of God (presumably some kind of angelic beings) loved the daughters of men, who conceived children through them. This must have involved some rather intimate touching, but we do not know the details. Isaiah's vision in the temple certainly had powerful tactile elements, but it was the live coal rather than the angel which touched the lips of the prophet (Isa. 6.6f.). Mark (1.13) tells us that when the temptations of Jesus were over, angels ministered to him, and in Luke (22.43) we read that in the garden of Gethsemane, when he was distressed in prayer, an angel of God appeared and strengthened him, but we do not know whether in either case the angels touched him.

To a blind person, this story of Elijah and the angel's touch has a peculiar beauty. Sighted people are often awoken by the morning light filling the room, or perhaps by light falling upon their faces. Blind people are woken, if not by an external signal such as an alarm clock or a radio clock, then by some internal mechanism; but the first sensation is always of touch. One becomes aware of the pillow, and then of one's position in the bed. Most blind people probably do what I do, stretch out a hand for the radio, the sound of which is equivalent to that rush of reality which comes to a sighted person when they open their eyes. The thought that one might be woken from sleep by the touch of an angel is very beautiful. The angel could have called Elijah's name, as so often happens in these magical encounters. The young child Samuel in his sleep heard his name being called. When Elijah was touched, was he startled? Did he jump up with the thought that Jezebel's soldiers were upon him? The reason we often wake sleeping people by calling their names is because it is startling to be touched in one's sleep, but the touch of the angel was different. We are not told that Elijah saw the angel when he woke up. Was there perhaps a memory of the brush of shimmering wings? Was there a brief glimpse, midway between waking and sleeping, of the kind of presence that even if it is real, you think you have dreamt it? Oh let me be touched in my sleep by angelic wings and be healed. 'And dost thou touch me afresh? Once again I feel thy finger and find thee.'[15]

A vision of God for partially-sighted people

> You shall see my back; but my face shall not be seen. (Ex. 33.23).

Many partially-sighted people can see bodies but not faces. There is a strange and beautiful story in Exodus which has a message for such people. Moses had asked God if he might see God's glory. God replied, 'You cannot see my face; for no one shall see me and live' (Ex. 33.20). In that case, we are all partially-sighted people before God, but with God it is not a case of absolutes. It is not a matter of either you have sight or you do not. Just because you cannot see the face of God, it does not mean that you cannot see God's glory.

> And the Lord continued, 'See, there is a place by me where you shall stand on the rock; and while my glory passes by I will put you in a cleft of the rock, and I will cover you with my hand until I have passed by; then I will take away

> my hand, and you shall see my back; but my face shall not
> be seen.' (vv. 21–23)

Because you cannot see the face, you are not banished from
the presence. There is a place for you. It is a place near God,
for you shall 'stand by me'. It is a secure place, so that although
you are only partly sighted, you need not have any sense of
insecurity. You shall stand upon the rock. There is a cleft in
the rock, and to protect you from the intense mystery while
God is passing by in his glory, God will put you there. It is a
little place, a narrow place, perhaps a place in which you often
feel confined and restricted. It is a dark place and the darkness
may be growing deeper, but perhaps it is God who has put
you in that narrow place and the darkness may be the shadow
of his hand protecting you from a glory, a beauty, which no
human person could endure. As the moment is passing, as the
presence is moving on, the hand will be lifted and you will
catch a glimpse of movement. It will be a shadowy movement,
without detail, so that you will hardly know what it was. You
will not have that sense of consulting face to face as sighted
people do. Nevertheless, what you dimly perceive will still be
glorious. It will be God's back turned towards you in mercy.

The voice of the good shepherd

> The sheep hear his voice. He calls his own sheep by name
> and leads them out. When he has brought out all his own,
> he goes ahead of them, and the sheep follow him because
> they know his voice. They will not follow a stranger, but
> they will run from him because they do not know the voice
> of strangers. (John 10.3–5)

Here at last, in this Gospel so thoroughly based upon the
contrast between light and darkness, we find a passage which
springs right out of the world of the blind: being familiar with
someone's voice, following a voice, being called by name –

these are daily experiences of great significance for blind
people. Whereas sighted people get to know someone by the
visual image of the face, blind people get to know someone by
the sound of the voice and the memory of the person's name.
This is why, especially in a crowded room where there are
many people, I like to be greeted by name. A sighted person
can tell from the eye contact and the body posture that he or
she is being addressed, but it is not so easy when you are blind.
I like the person to say, 'Hello, John', because then I know it
is me they are addressing. The anonymous unidentified voice
presents a problem. When, in the doctor's waiting room, the
receptionist calls out, 'Next!', I have to ask, 'Is it me?' but the
sighted person knows who it is because the receptionist glances
in his or her direction. Blind people love names, and voices
without names are often a problem. Many people expect to
be recognized merely by their voice as they say 'Hello' against
a background of crowd noise. I tell sighted people to remember
that it is like always speaking on the telephone. It is seldom
sufficient for somebody merely to say, 'Hello'. With your closest and dearest friends that is certainly enough, but usually
more is required, and preferably the person should say their
name.

> I am the gate. Whoever enters by me will be saved, and will
> come in and go out and find pasture. (John 10.9)

Doors are particularly important to blind people. I am walking
home late at night. It is pouring with rain but I dare not hurry
in case I miss the vital clue, the lamp-post which tells me my
house is near. I tap my cane along the low wall of the house
next door to me and turn left, walking down the slight incline
of the forecourt of my house. If I am very careful, and very
lucky, I get the angle just right. Somehow I hear the sound
echoing from the front of the house and can direct myself
perfectly towards the open porch; once, when I already had
the front door key in my hand, holding it in front of me as I

approached the house, it went straight into the keyhole. Often, however, I am not quite so accurate. I strike the bay window and wonder if it is the one on the left of the porch or the one on the other side. I go to the right: garbage cans. Okay, it must be left. Yes, here it is – the front door. All this time the rain is pouring down and since I am holding a cane and a briefcase I cannot manage an umbrella as well. Once inside the front door, I can relax. Going out means going into the potentially unknown.

Doors out are just as important as doors in, as you realize most vividly when negotiating your way in and out of unfamiliar public toilets. The vital thing is not to leave the perimeter. As you enter, you have to decide whether to keep to the right-hand wall or to the left. I choose right. Here is a towel dryer on the wall, and now a row of hand basins. Now a door into a cubicle? No, it turns out to be a door into a storeroom. Retrace, always keeping the wall on the right hand. There is another door. It is a cubicle, and there are six more cubicles. The angle of the wall turns left and now there are urinals. Remember the sequence: towel dryer, hand basins, storeroom, cubicles. Now I am leaving. I retrace my steps. Cubicles. Storeroom. Hand basins. I use one. Hand dryer. I go through the door. Something is wrong. This is not the place where I should be. Am I outside altogether or have I simply entered another room I had not noticed? I return and explore again. Urinals. More hand dryers. More hand basins. A door. I go through it and there is my friend, who says, 'You've been a long time.' It appears that there are two exit doors from this place. One leading here and the other leading out on to a different section altogether. Somehow I had confused them.

They will never perish. No one will snatch them out of my hand. What my Father has given me is greater than all else, and no one can snatch it out of the Father's hand. (John 10.28–9)

We notice here the powerful tactile imagery. I am held tightly by someone's hand. I need not fear falling off the platform at the railway station, or getting lost in the toilet, or being mugged. The person I am with is strong and can see trouble coming a long way off. My friend will know what to do and where to go if there are signs of trouble. No one can snatch me from his hand.

Blindness as a model for faith

Now faith is the assurance of things hoped for, the conviction of things not seen. (Heb. 11.1)

In a Bible mostly written with the assumptions of a sighted world, it is refreshing to find a long, famous and central passage which regards blindness as a model of faith. Certainly, blindness is not actually mentioned in Hebrews 11, but then neither is sight mentioned in many of the passages which take sight for granted. The point about this chapter is not only that it does not take sight for granted; it also works on the assumption that sight is at best irrelevant and at worst an impediment to faith.

The chapter begins with a ringing declaration. Faith has to do with what is not seen. Since a blind person can see nothing, the whole of the blind person's life is immediately oriented towards the life of faith. We sometimes say that seeing is believing, but the first verse of Hebrews 11 disowns that orientation. Most sighted people feel very uncertain in the dark, but here we are told that faith is an assurance, a confidence of what cannot be seen. It was by this, and not by their sight, that the fathers and mothers of the tradition of faith gained the approval of God (v. 2).

In a world where what is not seen is so often dominated, patronized, by that which sees and is seen, it is wonderful to read that in the order of creation the unseen things have priority over those which are seen (v. 3). In the song of creation in Genesis 1, the evening had priority over the morning in the synthesis of the day, and so here again we find that the seen things depend upon and grow out of the unseen things. Indeed, sight is very superficial. It is no more than surface deep, skin deep. Our lives are based upon foundations which are not seen, and even our bodies depend upon functions and organs which cannot normally be seen.

The first person to be mentioned by name in this chapter is Abel, who 'died, but through his faith he still speaks' (Heb. 11.4). To a person who reads with ears not eyes, all of the dead are still speaking. When I moved from reading print to listening to human or synthetic speech, the entire library of books turned into a world of speech. I realized that inscription is just a way of making speech permanent. Naturally, that very permanence removes it a good distance from speech, for the inscribed speech no longer depends upon its immediate context to be understood, whilst living speech grows out of a particular time and place. Just the same, when the books were turned back into speech, I found a new and intimate sense of companionship.

I often run my hands over the books on the shelf which are waiting to be read and imagine all of their various tongues and voices, some male, some female, some of people still living, some from people long since dead, and yet they will all utter their messages to me and I will spend hours in their company listening to them. It is true, in a way, that I cannot reply, but on the other hand, if I myself write something which is then turned into speech by some other blind person, I am contributing to the conversation which they started. Although they will not hear me reply to them, a third party, listening to both of us, will notice how I at least have reacted to the voices from the past. After all, looked at in this way the entire Bible is nothing but a wonderful medley of all kinds of voices, telling stories and singing psalms, voices which sometimes speak to each other and sometimes address me directly. One of the early Christians said that he much preferred the living voice to the written page,[16] and one of the great advantages of reading with your ears is that the written page turns back again into the living voice.

The next person to be mentioned is Enoch, who was blind as far as death was concerned, because he 'was taken up so that he should not see death' (Heb. 11.5, RSV) and, as the older Bibles translated, 'He was not; for God took him' (Gen. 5.24, AV). He was not. So often people who cannot see have that sense that they no longer exist, that they have become invisible. This is because, without eye contact, a sighted person does not feel easily in contact with the personality of the other. Only recently, when I remarked later on something said at the dinner table, my ten-year-old boy said with surprise, 'How did you know that?' When I reminded him that I also had been at dinner, he was surprised: 'I didn't see you!' Just so. To see a person is often to see the eyes of the person. A blind person is 'not found' (v. 5).

The next person to be mentioned is Noah who was 'warned by God about events as yet unseen' (v. 7). He believed although he could not see them.

Abraham behaved like a typical blind person, for 'he set out, not knowing where he was going' (v. 8). Sometimes when we are entering our church on a Sunday morning, Marilyn will say to me, 'Let's not sit in the same place.' I say to her, 'You choose.' I must say that, because to me all the pews are pretty well alike. It is difficult to tell one from another. Is this the same one we sat in last week or is it different? Of course, I am aware of how far we have walked down the aisle and whether we have turned corners and so on, but it takes me some time to realize, as the choir or other music gets going, that we are nearer to the front, or over to one side. This is even more true when you are being taken somewhere by car. You have a sense of how long the journey was, but where is the place? You are told the name of the place. Is the place the name?

When we come to the description of Abraham and Sarah

and their descendants, there is one description for sighted people and another for blind people. On the one hand, their descendants were to be 'as many as the stars of heaven', and on the other hand, 'as the innumerable grains of sand by the seashore' (v. 12). All the people mentioned so far were a bit like partially-sighted people. They saw the promise, as it were, from a distance (v.13). They saw it through clouds and mist, as something appearing, perhaps looming up, and yet they could not be quite sure of it. Nevertheless, they were sure enough to base their lives on it.

This is why, when it comes to blind people, 'God is not ashamed to be called their God' (v. 16). For 'he has prepared a city for them' (v. 16) where there will be no darkness and no light of the sun, but a city beyond light and darkness, rejoicing in the presence of God alone (Rev. 21.23).

The next two people to be mentioned were both blind. 'Isaac invoked blessings for the future on Jacob and Esau' (Heb. 11.20), and 'Jacob, when dying, blessed each of the sons of Joseph' (v. 21). Each of those incidents refers to the time in their lives when they had become blind.

Now, in the reference to Moses as a baby, we are told that 'they saw that the child was beautiful' (v. 23). This certainly is a sighted person's response, although in a sense blind people may also see that a child is beautiful. However, my point is not that everything in this chapter has blind people in mind, but merely that when it is read by a blind person, certain features of it stand out and speak rather vividly. Later, we are told of Moses that 'he persevered as though he saw him who is invisible' (v. 27). In the presence of God, we are all blind, because God is invisible.

Then we come to the great list of heroes of faith, amongst whom there is place for Samson, who 'won strength out of weakness' (v. 34) and is a blind person's hero. Samson, in his blindness, 'suffered mocking and flogging, and even chains and imprisonment' (v. 36).

When the author has finished this survey of the heroes of faith, he or she concludes that, fine and heroic though these people were, they will not be complete without us. That reminds us that since the life of faith is particularly symbolized in blindness, and since blind people carry the stamp of the likeness of God in a very special way, sighted people cannot be complete without blind people. The life of faith is made up of this variety and all varieties.

Thomas: A blessing for blindness

Although you have not seen him, you love him; and even though you do not see him now, you believe in him and rejoice with an indescribable and glorious joy. (I Peter 1.8)

Have you believed because you have seen me? Blessed are those who have not seen and yet have come to believe. (John 20.29)

Let us hear what gracious words are spoken to us as blind Christians and as people of faith who respond to God in any tradition. 'Blessed are those who have not seen and yet have come to believe.' Usually this passage is thought to refer to people who were absent, who had had no opportunity to check up on the stories for themselves. It is a story for second and third generation Christians, now separated from the event by time. However, it is certainly a saying also to be received by people who cannot see and have never seen. A special blessing is reserved for them.

Nevertheless, we must ask whether there is not a profound connection between seeing someone and loving someone. Do not sighted people treasure the photographs of their loved ones? Do they not display them on the walls of their homes and their offices? True, people make friends and even fall in love and marry through the Internet, but one of the first things they do when they are becoming friendly is to exchange photographs, isn't it?

A blind date is supposed to be exciting, but it would not be so exciting if, when you had met your date, you found that he or she was blind, or that you yourself, being blind, could form no instant impressions of your partner. I once read a story in which two people meet over a meal. The story describes their emotions and their gradual exploration of each other. They are an attractive young couple and we wonder what will happen. The punch line comes when the author reveals that underneath the table are two guide dogs. We are then supposed to think how tragic it is, that they are unable to appreciate each other's attractiveness, or that, in spite of everything we have got to know about them, there is a pathos and loss about the fact that each is blind to the other.

Does it really matter? It probably matters more to the sighted partner than to the blind one. There is a terrible loss in being unable to display yourself attractively to someone you love, or someone whom you want to love you. All your beauty, handsomeness, stylish clothing, careful manicure, attractive hair cut, all for nothing. The person you love can only respond to your voice. As far as relative strangers are concerned, it is perfectly possible to flirt with the voice only, but it is easier to flirt with the eyes, if one wants to flirt and has eyes. On the other hand, you hear stories of people who met each other more or less by accident on the telephone and fell in love. Certainly you can fall in love with someone's voice. In times of intimacy, blindness is not so important. Darkness is the time of closeness, warmth and intimacy. It is in the in-between stages, the early expressions of attraction, that sight seems to be so important.

If we turn to the parent–child relationship, people often ask me whether I have any visual memories of my children. They seem to expect a difference between the older children, of whom I have dim visual memories, and the younger ones, whom I have never seen. To me, however, this so-called difference is trivial and irrelevant. You do not cease to love just because you go blind. Indeed, there is a strange and exhilarating joy in loving and being loved when you cannot see. Just because the intermediate stages are taken away, there is a breathless rush of givenness, a sense of having been graciously presented with the person of the beloved. I may read about and imagine many people who were dead long ago and whom thus I cannot see. But my loved ones, my dear ones, are my contemporaries. I cannot see them either, but their presence conveys the concrete immediacy of love.

It is something to do with the connection between love and life. I love to embrace the trunk of this tree, to feel its amazing intricacy, its strength and how it vibrates in the breeze. I love to pick up this wonderfully shaped piece of glasswork, to hold it in my hand, but the tree and the glasswork do not respond to me. They do not move at my movements. When I put my hand underneath the kitten and lift it on to my knees, however, it moves! It responds to my action. It is because blindness eliminates a good deal of the sense of place that this immediacy is so impressive. To a blind person, there is nothing and then there is presence. First you are nowhere. Then you step into my arms. It is this quality of being surprised by presence that lends such a particular joy to blindness.

At this point, sighted people always want to ask whether it would not be even better if one could see. However, that question must be put aside. It is purely theoretical, but love is tangible. Of course, there are many wonderful delicacies about the relationship between sight and love, but it is also true that there are treasures of darkness.

When it comes to loving God, we must remember that in God's presence everyone is blind. The distinction between being sighted and being blind disappears in the presence of God. This is something to which sighted people as well as blind people can look forward. God, we are told, 'dwells in unapproachable light, whom no one has ever seen, or can see' (I Tim. 6.16). If the light is unapproachable, if it is impenetrable, it might as well be darkness. There is darkness visible and there is brightness invisible. In these images, the blind God of blind people and the sighted God of sighted people are overcome, are transcended.

7

Jesus

Jesus: The face and the name

When we think of people from the past, does a visual image come into our minds? In the case of deceased relatives, the photograph hanging on the wall is probably the way we invoke their memory. With people further back in history, this is not necessarily the case. There are, no doubt, certain historical figures who do immediately convey a visual image, for example the kings and queens of modern England, whose faces are familiar from postage stamps. Many famous people from the past are associated with a particular object or posture, such as Napoleon with his hand inside his jacket, or Nelson holding up the telescope to his blind eye. The face, however, is seldom visualized, unless it is associated with a particularly famous portrait. If we go back into the ancient world, there are lots of famous people who do not have faces at all. Homer is wearing a toga and sandals, perhaps with a bald head, but it is more difficult to visualize his features.

It is important for Christian faith that Jesus lived in a culture that possessed the art of writing but was without photography, television or video. The written word requires interpretation and has all sorts of double and hidden meanings which the concrete nature of sight tends to dispel. The many-sided ambiguity of Jesus as depicted in the four Gospels and the writings of Paul would present a different problem for faith if original sketches of his face were available. He is present to us in words but not in images. 'Although you have not seen him, you love

him; and even though you do not see him now, you believe in
him' (I Peter 1.8). The sighted believer building up a relationship with Jesus does not start with the visual image and make
it the core to which everything else is attached, as happens
with contemporaries. Sighted people have to work just like
blind people, through making associations with the name itself.

There are, of course, innumerable later artists' impressions
of the face of Christ. These are, if anything, a distraction to
the Christian believer, who is required to know Jesus Christ
though his word and not in the flesh. 'Blessed are those who
have not seen and yet have come to believe' (John 20.29).

It is thus understandable to a blind person that in the New
Testament there is such an emphasis upon the name of Jesus.
We are baptized into the name, we call upon the name, and it
is at the name that every knee shall bow. The blind person
always works with names, not faces.

Jesus the sighted prophet

> Let them alone; they are blind guides of the blind. And if
> one blind person guides another, both will fall into a pit.
> (Matt. 15.14)

Many of the sayings of Jesus indicate that his outlook is that
of a sighted person addressing sighted people.

> You are the light of the world. A city built on a hill cannot
> be hid. No one after lighting a lamp puts it under the bushel
> basket, but on the lamp-stand, and it gives light to all in
> the house. In the same way, let your light shine before others,
> so that they may see your good works and give glory to
> your Father in heaven. (Matt. 5.14–16)

On the other hand, the previous verse suggests experiences
very familiar to blind people. 'You are the salt of the earth;
but if salt has lost its taste, how can its saltiness be restored?

It is no longer good for anything, but is thrown out and trampled under foot' (Matt. 5.13).

The visual theme re-emerges in verse 28:

> Everyone who looks at a woman with lust has already committed adultery with her in his heart. If your right eye causes you to sin, tear it out and throw it away; it is better for you to lose one of your members than for your whole body to be thrown into hell. (Matt. 5: 28f.)

This is obviously a sighted person's view of sexual desire, and the comment about plucking your eye out should it 'cause you to sin' suggests that blind people are incapable of sexual sin, or are at least protected by blindness against this particular kind of visual offence. Once again, however, this is balanced by the following verse, which is more tactile: 'And if your right hand causes you to sin, cut it off and throw it away; it is better for you to lose one of your members than for your whole body to go into hell' (v. 30). This can be compared with the hands that see and know in Matt. 6.3: 'When you give alms, do not let your left hand know what your right hand is doing, so that your alms may be done in secret.' Here, hands are compared to eyes or are given the properties of eyes. How can you fail to know what your hands are doing? You are always aware of the position of one hand, unless it has been anaesthetized. You cannot close down a hand, but you can close an eye. When you shut your left eye you might say that it does not know or see what your right eye sees.

In this figure of speech, the hands are spoken of as if they were eyes, one of which could be shut. When I was a child we sometimes played a game whose purpose was to create a situation in which you could not tell one hand from the other, or your hands from those of other people. Three or four children would make a big pile with their hands, interlocking them and sandwiching each hand in-between the hands of others, and then merely by looking you had to identify which was your own finger. It was hard to tell: you could not touch the pile of fingers because your hands were in the pile, and you were not allowed to move. This was an amusing way of preventing your left hand from knowing what your right hand was doing. Of course, in the end it was always impossible to prevent giving a twitch to the chosen finger, but then there were always arguments about whether that was the finger you had in mind or not. This was obviously a game which only sighted children could play.

In verse 5 we return from this strange visual, tactile image to the world of sight. The hypocrites mentioned here loved to pray standing on the street corners, 'so that they may be seen'.

We move away from the visual world again when we come to the Lord's Prayer (Matt. 6.9–13). The prayer could well be said by a blind person, since it contains a request to be led, or rather not to be led, into danger or trial. There is nothing in the prayer that a blind person cannot experience, except perhaps the idea of the sky or heaven. The importance of the name, eating bread and being close to one's father – these are all within the blind experience.

When we come to the hypocrites who 'disfigure their faces so as to show others that they are fasting' (v. 16), we are back in the sighted world.

> The eye is the lamp of the body. So, if your eye is healthy, your whole body will be full of light; but if your eye is unhealthy, your whole body will be full of darkness. If then the light in you is darkness, how great is the darkness! (Matt. 6: 22–23)

Here we sense the instinctive horror a sighted person has of being plunged into that darkness. A blind person does not feel full of darkness, but full of normality.

This describes a culture of appearances, where what matters is what looks right. Indeed, the Sermon on the Mount as a whole could be read as a criticism of this world of sight, the world where what matters is what things look like. When Jesus invites sighted people to 'Look at the birds of the air!' (v. 26), he is, by implication, saying, 'Notice the things which you have never really noticed before.' When we come to the famous words, 'Consider the lilies of the field . . . even Solomon in all his glory was not clothed like one of these' (vv. 28–29), the criticism of the sighted world reaches a climax.

> Why do you see the speck in your neighbour's eye, but do not notice the log in your own eye? Or how could you say to your neighbour, 'Let us take the speck out of your eye,' while the log is in your own eye? You hypocrite, first take the log out of your own eye, and then you will see clearly to take the speck out of your neighbour's eye. (Matt. 7.3–5)

Jesus continues to speak as a sighted person, whether telling other sighted people not to be so worried about their appearance, or in sharp criticism of the way that sighted people tend to be preoccupied with the details of the appearance and behaviour of others. The same warning is to be found in verse 15: 'Beware of false prophets, who come to you in sheep's clothing but inwardly are ravenous wolves.'

'Ask, and it will be given to you; search, and you will find; knock, and the door will be opened for you' (Matt. 7.7). These words must ring true in the ears of every blind person. How often do we ask; how often we wait hesitating on railway platforms and at street crossings wondering if it will be possible to ask someone. How often have I stood on a deserted platform at a railway station, with the train about to depart, a platform alteration just announced and no one around to give assistance! The last time that happened, I held my white cane in the air and swung it backwards and forwards over my head shouting out 'Hoy!' A voice called from the opposite platform, 'Are you okay?' As soon as the porter realized what I wanted, he came hurrying across to me and guided me safely to my train.

Seek and you shall find. Certainly, as a blind person I do a great deal of seeking and not quite so much finding, but the word of Jesus is not exactly about my life; it is the place where my life is touched by the promise. Ask, seek, knock! All these things a blind person does often. When we are told a few verses later to 'Enter through the narrow gate; for the gate is wide and the road is easy that leads to destruction, and there are many who take it' (Matt. 7.13), we can again see that this is the world from a sighted person's point of view. For a sighted person, a wide gate is an easy gate. For a blind person, a wide gate is a difficult gate because you do not know when you have gone through it. It is the narrow gate, where you can touch the sides and know exactly where it is and when you have gone through it, that blind people like. I do not like it when both the double doors are propped open on hot days. For me, the doors are not there. It makes it more difficult for me to know exactly where I am. So the advice to enter it by the narrow gate is one which blind people can easily follow and, as the verse says, there are not many that go that way.

In the Sermon on the Mount we find the sighted prophet speaking in three ways. First, he speaks to the sighted world in ways that seem to share the sighted prejudice against the blind world. Second, the prophet attacks the sighted culture, exposing the superficiality of judgements based upon appearances. Finally, he includes the blind world by referring to so many experiences with which blind people would be familiar. It is in this mode that the sermon concludes:

> The rain fell, the floods came, and the winds blew and beat on that house, but it did not fall, because it had been founded on rock. (Matt. 7.25)

Sometimes when I am sitting in my rain-room at home, I wonder if the next gust will blow the light sheets of plastic roofing completely off, and what a mess it would be then! As I hear the torrents of water pouring down the side of the house from the flooded storm pipes and the overflowing gutters, while the walls vibrate with the shocks of thunder, I wonder if I would notice if the house very slowly started to slide down the hill towards the stream at the foot of the garden. Would I be aware of the rumbling? Then I get up and walk around the rest of the house. Everywhere the windows are rattling and, up in the attic, there is a steady drumming on the skylight windows. Otherwise the house is still, steady and patient. Tony and Geoff, who built the extensions, dug deep and well. I remember lowering my white cane into the trench at the time. I could not touch the bottom. They cleared away the surface soil and went down until they reached the rock.

Jesus as a tactile person

He stretched out his hand and touched him. (Matt. 8.3)

He touched her hand. (Matt. 8.15)

There are many references like this that show Jesus touching people. Several of them are associated with healing, which means that we think of the touch of Jesus as intending to do something and do not often ask whether Jesus actually liked touching people and enjoyed being touched.

He was often surrounded by crowds, and although it is true that sometimes he sought peace and solitude, there is nothing to indicate that he did not enjoy being in the company of people, even when they pressed all around him. When a woman with a haemorrhage touched the edge of his cloak and Jesus felt it, he asked who touched him. The disciples were surprised and pointed out that everyone was crowding around him, so how could he possibly ask which particular one had touched him (Mark 5.30f.).

When the mothers bring their children to be blessed by Jesus, he does not merely lay his hands upon them. He takes them in his arms (Mark 10.16). This incident is often used to prove that Jesus loved children, but it also seems to suggest that Jesus liked holding children. This suggests that he was a tactile sort of person.

When Jesus is at dinner in the house of Simon the Pharisee, a woman comes in and anoints the feet of Jesus with some fragrant ointment. Then she begins to cry and to wipe his feet with her hair. Since she has rather a bad reputation, some of the people sitting around the table begin to criticize him, saying that if Jesus really is a prophet, he would know what sort of woman it is who is now touching him. Touching him she certainly is, and he feels the warm tears as they fall. To have one's feet dried with the soft hair of a woman who, whatever her reputation, is probably very beautiful, is a tactile sensation that most men would enjoy. Far from trying to stop her, Jesus defends her action by saying that she has done a beautiful thing to him. He speaks tenderly to her, saying that her action will never be forgotten (Luke 7.37–50).

When Jesus was sitting with his closest friends at the table in the upper room, the night on which he was betrayed, he must have felt particularly isolated and full of foreboding. However, the disciple that Jesus loved leant right up close to him during the meal. Yes, there is no doubt that Jesus welcomed the intimacy of touch (John 13.23, 25).

After his resurrection, there are two incidents which help us to keep in touch with this tactile man. Luke tells us that when he appeared to his disciples in the upper room on the Sunday night, they were afraid because they thought he was a ghost. He asked for something to eat, to prove that he was a real human person, and invited them to touch him (Luke 24.39f.). Moreover, when doubting Thomas saw him a week later, he was also invited to stretch out his hand and touch Jesus (John 20.27). To a certain extent, of course, these details are recorded in order to make the point that the resurrection was real, but at the same time, we may believe that to touch Jesus was a perfectly natural continuation of the way in which he had always been with them.

There is one striking moment when Jesus refuses to be

touched. John reports that when Mary recognizes him in the garden, having previously thought he was the gardener and comes toward him at the sound of her name, Jesus restrains her with the words, 'Do not hold on to me' (John 20.17). Why does he invite Thomas to touch him but tells Mary not to cling on to him? It is surely because the invitation to Thomas (an invitation which, by the way, Thomas does not accept), is offered as a proof to someone who doubts, but Mary, once she hears him speak her name, is no longer in doubt. Her touch would be an embrace. This is why he adds, 'because I have not yet ascended'. The embrace of Mary would restrain him. It would hold him to the earth, but his ascension must not be delayed.

'Blind' as a term of abuse

Woe to you, blind guides! (Matt. 23.16)

It is sad and distressing to note that the word 'blind' as a term of abuse is attributed to Jesus in St Matthew's Gospel. Following this text, we then have, 'You blind fools . . .' (v. 17), 'How blind you are!' (v. 19), 'You blind guides! You strain out a gnat but swallow a camel! (v. 24), and 'You blind Pharisee! First clean the inside of the cup, so that the outside also may become clean' (v. 26).

These comments do seem to be particularly true of how the behaviour of some blind people would look. Let us take the idea that you never know what you are eating: you spit out a gnat and then you swallow a camel. Only recently, at a rather formal university dinner, I managed to fork several nice pieces of tomato, but the next one, although more or less the same shape and size, turned out to be a segment of lemon. As I bit into it, something snapped and went all gooey. No longer caring about what things look like to others, I hastily retrieved it from my mouth, laid it on my side plate and examined it. Neatly balanced on the lemon slice, as if deliberately to trap me, was a little pat of butter, wrapped up in paper. I had bitten right through it into the lemon and had a mouthful of extremely sharp lemon-flavoured butter in my mouth. It only took a moment to empty this out into the paper napkin conveniently provided. On these occasions, I remember the rebuke offered to Dr Johnson when he hastily removed a round, hot potato out of his mouth. 'You looked a real fool doing that!' said the person next to him at the table. 'Yes, perhaps,' he replied, 'but I'd have look an even bigger fool if I hadn't!'

The same is true of the inside of the cup. How do I know if the inside is clean? Only by touching it, and then it needs washing anyway. In my office, the used cups and mugs are on the windowsill and the clean, washed ones are in the cupboard. Anything which is on the windowsill, I wash. Sometimes a kindly friend, noticing the piled up mugs, washes them for me and puts them back on the windowsill. Not noticing this until the next day, when they are cool and dry, I go and wash them all again. There is no other way to be sure. Yes, my Lord, I am a blind fool and sometimes I find indeed, as you say, that I have washed the outside of the mug and left a little bit of hardened coffee at the bottom. If you had coffee with me, Jesus, would you have confidence as I made the coffee? Would you watch me anxiously as I went to my clean cupboard to get a couple of mugs, as I took some paper tissues from a nice clean box and carefully rubbed the cups inside and outside? Would you watch me carefully in case I put my finger into your mug as I poured the boiling water in? Well, there is no need to be afraid. I only use the 'Ouch!' method when I am by myself. When I am with you, I ask you to tell me when.

A great deal of our colourful, ordinary, daily language is taken from the appearance and behaviour of disabled people. However, we sophisticated people no longer say of a person with personality or mental problems that he or she is 'bonkers', and we no longer refer to psychiatric hospitals as 'nut-houses'. We prevent our children from saying, 'You dumb spazzo' when someone is clumsy, because we know that children should not be encouraged to sneer at spastic children. In spite of all this, I hear my sophisticated colleagues on examination boards referring to 'blind marking', and that they drove their cars up 'a blind alley', and after a party someone may well remark that he was 'blind drunk'. All these expressions denigrate the blind condition by suggesting, in that humorous and familiar way which is the mark of true prejudice, that we blind people are ignorant, that our lives are going nowhere, and that our behaviour makes other people think we are always intoxicated. People who would not dream of using such insulting expressions about a person from a different ethnic or racial group, are not embarrassed to use expressions which demean disabled people. Unfortunately, my Lord Jesus, my gentle master, does not, in this matter, provide us with a satisfactory model.

Jesus blindfolded

When the men had come to him, they said, 'John the Baptist has sent us to you to ask, "Are you the one who is to come, or are we to wait for another?"' Jesus had just then cured many people of diseases, plagues, and evil spirits, and had given sight to many who were blind. And he answered them, 'Go and tell John what you have seen and heard: the blind receive their sight, the lame walk, the lepers are cleansed, the deaf hear, the dead are raised, the poor have good news brought to them. And blessed is anyone who takes no offence at me. (Luke 7.20–23)

In the earlier books of the Bible, we are sometimes offered acceptance and inclusion as an alternative to restoration of sight. In the ministry of Jesus this alternative does not appear. The only thing to do with blind people is to restore their sight. Just after Matthew's account of the cleansing of the temple, we are told that, 'The blind and the lame came to him in the temple, and he cured them' (Matt. 21.14). On the whole, the people seem to share this view, for 'the crowd was amazed when they saw the mute speaking, the maimed whole, the lame walking, and the blind seeing. And they praised the God of Israel' (Matt. 15.31). Indeed, Jesus speaks of the restoration of the sight of blinded people as being an integral part of his mission, when he quotes the words from the book of Isaiah in his address in the synagogue at Nazareth:

> The spirit of the Lord is upon me, because he has anointed me to bring good news to the poor. He has sent me to proclaim release to the captives and recovery of sight to the blind, to let the oppressed go free, to proclaim the year of the Lord's favour. (Luke 4.18f.)

This raises the question whether a blind person can become a disciple of Jesus. We know that ordinary working people follow him, like the fishermen from Galilee, and he also accepts people from unpopular occupations, like Matthew the tax-gatherer. Even a member of a rather doubtful group of political radicals is admitted to his inner circle, Simon the Zealot. Women, even women who have had a shady past, are regular members of his team (Luke 8.2), but there is no blind person, and the context of the Gospels as a whole compels us to wonder whether this is possible. People would ask why this man who restores the sight of so many blind people does not or cannot restore the sight of so-and-so, his chosen disciple. Would not the opponents of Jesus say – as they said of Lazarus, 'Could not he who opened the eyes of the blind man have kept this man from dying?' (John 11.37) – 'Could not this man, who opened the eyes of those who were not even his disciples, have opened the eyes of this man who follows him so closely?' Would not the other disciples find the presence of a blind disciple a continual embarrassment, since people would ask them 'What about him then?'?

If I could not have been a blind disciple then, how can I be a blind disciple now? If the disciples would have been embar-

rassed then, does it not justify the church members of today
who are embarrassed to find a blind member of their church?
Of course, we could join those who say that the age of miracles
has passed, and it is certainly clear that blind Christians would
feel more uncomfortable in the churches which practise a char-
ismatic healing ministry on the model that Jesus understood
literally, than in the churches of today which emphasize that
the greatest miracle is when the gospel is proclaimed to the
poor. Suppose that I was approached by Jesus today? Would
he be able to accept me today as a blind person?

At this point we must give a new twist to the statement of
Jesus when he says, 'And blessed is anyone who takes no
offence at me'. Presumably, Jesus means that John the Baptist
in prison would have been offended if he had heard that Jesus
had not been healing blind people, since that is what the Messiah was supposed to do. For us today, it is different. We tend
to be offended because he does heal blind people, and we ask
why it is that he is not able to accept blind people amongst
his disciples. That feeling of offence, often not expressed or
barely conscious, runs right through the spiritual life of many
Christian blind people. Rather than feel offended at Jesus, we
Christian blind people tend to turn it back upon ourselves and
feel offended at ourselves for having such thoughts, or even
perhaps for being blind. Rather than feel ashamed of Jesus we
prefer to feel ashamed of our blindness. Yet the word of Jesus
remains, not only to John the Baptist in prison but to his
followers today in blindness: 'Blessed are you if you are not
offended by me.'

There are three passages which hint at a different approach.
In Luke 14 Jesus says:

> When you give a luncheon or a dinner, do not invite your
> friends or your brothers or your relatives or rich neighbours,
> in case they may invite you in return, and you would be
> repaid. But when you give a banquet, invite the poor, the
> crippled, the lame, and the blind. And you will be blessed,

because they cannot repay you, for you will be repaid at the resurrection of the righteous. (Luke 14.12–15)

This is illustrated in the parable which follows. When a rich man's guests did not come to his feast, 'the owner of the house became angry and said to his slave, "Go out at once into the streets and lanes of the town and bring in the poor, the crippled, the blind, and the lame"' (Luke 14.21).

These passages have a double edge. On the one hand, it is evident that Jesus does not think that the poor and the disabled have anything to contribute to the feast. The point about inviting them is that it is an act of pure unselfishness since you have nothing to gain from them. To this we might reply that the conversation of the poor and the disabled is sometimes a bit more interesting than the table talk of your relatives and rich neighbours. Indeed, disabled people are often famous for their conversational powers and, along with the poor, they often present a different view of life's experiences which is not only challenging but refreshing to many people who have never thought of these things before. What are we to say about this story in the light of the many parents who have been discouraged at first when they realized they had a disabled child but found later that they received more blessings from this child than from all the rest?

The more positive side of the story is the realization that blind people are at least accepted around the table. This is one of the few examples of inclusion rather than healing which we find in the Gospels. The blessing which they give to the householder is nothing but their presence. Like St Paul, they have nothing to offer but their weakness, nothing to boast of but their infirmities (II Cor. 12.5).

The second hint comes from the very end of the Fourth Gospel. Having challenged his love for him, Jesus says to Peter,

when you were younger, you used to fasten your own belt and go wherever you wished. But when you grow old you

will stretch out your hands, and someone else will fasten a
belt around you and take you where you do not wish to go.
(John 21.18)

The Gospel continues, 'He said this to indicate the kind of
death by which he would glorify God' (v. 19). However, we
may believe that this is not the only reason Jesus says these
words, or not the only meaning that we can receive from them
today. Jesus contrasts the independence and freedom of the
fully able-bodied person with the constriction, dependence and
lack of autonomy of the disabled person. Somebody else will
have to dress you: somebody else will have to choose your
clothes: somebody else will have to take you shopping. You
will be taken to places you do not want to go to. I remember
once at a meeting asking someone to take me to the bookstore.
'With pleasure,' replied my new acquaintance, and I put my
finger on her elbow. Leaving the room, the sound of conversation died away and we walked along corridors and through
other rooms until at last we entered a shop. 'Here you are,'
my new-found friend said, 'This is the bookroom.' I had been
taken right out of the meeting into the regular bookshop
attached to the building. I explained that what I had really
wanted was to see the display of literature in the lecture room
itself and, laughing, we retraced our steps. This is a little incident but it illustrates a big problem. What with misunderstandings, the inability to realize exactly where you are going, and
sometimes an excessive goodwill on the part of strangers, blind
people often find themselves in places where they did not expect
to be. Then Jesus said to Peter, 'Follow me' (v. 19).

It does not matter that Peter loses his independence and
becomes, in a sense, disabled by suffering. In spite of that, or
perhaps just because of that, he is able to follow Jesus. That
destiny is part of his discipleship.

The following words are equally significant. Peter notices
the disciple who has been leaning close to Jesus at the last
supper. He says to Jesus, 'Lord, what about him?' Jesus said

to him, 'If it is my will that he remains until I come, what is that to you? Follow me!' (v. 22).

'It is no business of yours,' says Jesus, 'how this person's discipleship will unfold. Just mind your own business and get on with your own responsibilities.' This could be the reply of Jesus to the people we imagined before, asking him why he does not heal this blind disciple while he heals others who are not his disciples. His answer is that he calls each person to his or her own unique discipleship. What business is it of yours if I am called to a discipleship of blindness? What business is it of mine if you are called to the discipleship of a sighted life? Let us each follow him in accordance with the path to which we have been called.

The third hint which helps us not to be offended at Jesus occurs in Mark 14.65: 'Some began to spit on him, to blindfold him, and to strike him, saying to him "Prophesy!" The guards also took him over and beat him.'

There are only two places in the Bible where blindness is simulated by being blindfolded. King Ahab spares the life of the defeated king of Damascus, Ben-hadad, allowing him to get up into his own chariot and describing him as his own brother. While the soldiers on each side perish, the two kings are preparing a comfortable exit. I Kings 20.38–43 describes how an unknown prophet, who has persuaded a fellow prophet to strike him and wound him, is standing with his head bandaged waiting for the chariot of the king to pass by. Rather in the style of the prophet Nathan, the unknown prophet tells the king how he himself has let his prisoner go. When the king replies that his punishment should be as he himself had expected, the unknown prophet whips off the bandage and says, in effect, 'Well, it's you I am talking about really!' The idea is that if King Ahab had recognized the bandaged, wounded war veteran earlier, he would not have walked into the trap set for him. In the story of King Ahab, a blindfolded prophet confronts a king; in the story of Jesus, a blindfolded prophet confronts his tormentors. King Ahab's unknown prophet voluntarily blindfold himself in order to deceive the king, but in the Gospel of St Mark the prophet is blindfolded by his tormentors in order to tease him about his prophetic powers.

During this period of humiliation and mockery, Jesus understood what it is like as a blind person to be in a state of ignorance. 'Who struck you?' (Luke 22.64). It is in this sadistic game of blind man's buff that blind people can most readily identify with the sufferings of Jesus Christ. It is because, however briefly, he shares our condition, undergoing a mockery and a humiliation which few of us have had to undergo, that we cannot be offended at him. Dear Master, it is all one to me whether you restore my sight or call me in my blindness to follow you. I do not ask you to heal me but only that if you call me to follow you in blindness, you will hold my hand.

The anger of Jesus

> He looked around at them with anger; he was grieved at their hardness of heart and said to the man, 'Stretch out your hand.' (Mark 3.5)

This is one of the very few places where Jesus is portrayed as being angry, and it is provoked by the attitude of the people around him towards disability. A disabled man has come into the synagogue on the Sabbath day. The building is packed with well-educated, religious people who have come to see whether Jesus is doing or saying anything illegal. They watch closely to see whether Jesus will heal the man, which is apparently forbidden on the Sabbath day.

When Jesus realizes what is going on and notices the disabled man, he calls him to come right out in front of everybody. This is a direct challenge. Jesus could pretend that he has not noticed the man, who is probably sitting at the back anyway. He could get someone to read a passage from the Bible or sing something while he thinks about it. He could take the disabled man on to the porch or even tell him to come back later.

When the disabled man is standing out in front of the whole congregation, Jesus asks them a question: 'Is it lawful to do good or to do evil on the sabbath, to save life or to kill it?' (v. 4). This brings a complete silence. Nobody moves. No one says a word. This makes Jesus angry. Even with the disabled man standing right there in front of them, probably shuffling nervously and trying to conceal his withered hand, there is no one to have pity on him, no one who puts the welfare and healing of the disabled person before religious principle. The congregation cannot defend themselves, but they are too hard of heart to feel shame. Turning to the disabled man, Jesus says, 'Stretch out your hand,' and the man is immediately restored.

Still today the angry Christ throws his challenge at us. His anger still grows hot at the people who think that while it is bad luck to be disabled, it is a more important religious duty to hold to your principles.

The opposite of anger is not love, as many people think, but bitterness. Anger that is repressed turns into bitterness, not into love. Bitterness may be driven out by love, but only when that love is love for others, not love for oneself, and when the love is energetic enough to feel anger on behalf of others. This is how a disabled person can avoid feelings of bitterness. After all, what is bitterness? It is a feeling of disappointment together with a sense of injustice. Moreover, bitterness is experienced when disappointment and injustice have endured over a period of time without relief. You do not become bitter overnight. Bitterness comes with reflection. At first, in the disappointment of your loss, you are shocked, perhaps numbed, and you look for help or relief. You expect the loss to be followed by some kind of recompense or adjustment. Slowly you realize that the loss is permanent and then the sense of outrage or of having been the victim of an injustice may slowly form.

How could anyone dare, you say to yourself, to strike me down with cancer while my children are still young? How could anyone dare to inflict an accident upon me when I am becoming so successful at football? How could anyone dare to give me such beautiful children and then take away my ability to see their faces?

We easily personify the source of this outrage. One of my friends, a woman in the prime of life with four young children, was diagnosed as having cancer and four weeks later was dead. Her husband said to me, 'She was raped by cancer.' Such a reaction, to regard death as a rapist, is very understandable. However, especially if we feel that some human agency is at work in our loss and no reparation is offered, the sense of bitterness can grow deep with us.

We understand how this happens, but do we understand those occasions when it does not happen? How does it come about that some people experience loss, whether from human actions or from accidents, but do not become bitter? It is because, like Jesus, they become angry on behalf of others. Some strange, sublimating energy enables such people to transform the injury done to the self into a sense of the injustice done toward others. 'He took our infirmities and bore our diseases' (Matt. 8.17).

This saying, which Matthew quotes from Isa. 53.4, is not really fulfilled by the healing miracles of Jesus. Instead of bearing our diseases, he simply heals them. Nevertheless, when he shows compassion for a bereaved mother (Luke 7.13) or two blind men (Matt. 20.34), that must mean that he entertains a fellow-feeling, and when he groans with the sorrow of a bereaved sister and then weeps (John 11.35), he is doing more than simply healing; he is entering into the loss and bearing it.

Speaking of the suffering servant of God, Isaiah says,

> there were many who were astonished at him – so marred was his appearance, beyond human semblance, and his form beyond that of mortals. (Isa. 52.14)

> he had no form or majesty that we should look at him, nothing in his appearance that we should desire him. He

was despised and rejected by others; a man of suffering and acquainted with infirmity. (Isa. 53.2f.)

At the sight of God's disabled servant we might think that he is 'stricken, struck down by God, and afflicted' (Isa. 53.4) and then it would not be surprising if he felt bitterness, and that we who identify with him should share his bitterness. Then we realize the truth: 'surely he has borne our infirmities and carried our diseases' (v. 4).

How does he bear our infirmities and carry our diseases? First, by entering into our disabilities in compassion, then by going beyond compassion to anger on our behalf, and finally by becoming one of us. 'I am poured out like water, and all my bones are out of joint; my heart is like wax; it is melted within my breast; my mouth is dried up' (Ps. 22.14f.). He takes upon himself the frustrations and humiliations of blindness (Luke 22.64), is unable to carry heavy weights (Luke 23.26), and finally loses all mobility in the most painful way (Luke 23.33). Indeed, we may say of him that he starts by healing us in anger, and finishes by participating in our lives through love.

It is his anger which leads him to the cross. It is that refusal to accept injustice, that flaming indignation at the hardness of the human heart, which leads him to his final act of defiance, that physical identification with disabled people and that moral identification with thieves and robbers. It is through participating in his anger that we ourselves escape bitterness. We turn our anger out towards the injustices of the world. Though disabled, we take upon ourselves the disabilities of others, thus becoming agents of change and followers of him who 'took our infirmities and bore our diseases' (Matt. 8.17).

Notes

Chapter 1

1. The Hebrew word is *rakkot*, which often means tender, timid or delicately nurtured. Although the NRSV translates 'Leah's eyes were lovely', it seems better to follow the RSV, which says, 'Leah's eyes were weak'. This is consistent with the ironic humour of the story, in which the tricky Jacob is himself tricked. There was something about the eyes that made her unattractive – maybe she was short-sighted.
2. Lad (AV, RSV) or attendant (NRSV).
3. The RSV reading of 16.28, referred to in a footnote in the NRSV.
4. J. C. Dancy, *The Shorter Books of the Apocrypha*, Cambridge: CUP 1972; and Frank Zimmerman, *The Book of Tobit*, New York: Harper 1958.
5. Some of the texts say that he was fifty-eight.
6. RSV.

Chapter 2

7. John M. Hull, *The Hellenistic Magic and the Synoptic Tradition*, London: SCM Press 1974.
8. E. S. Johnson, 'Mark VIII: 22–26. The Blind Man from Bethsaida', *New Testament Studies* 25, pp. 370–83.
9. E. S. Johnson, 'Mark 10: 46–52: Blind Bartimaeus', *Catholic Biblical Quarterly* 40, 1978.
10. Dennis Hamm, 'Paul's Blindness and Its Healing: Clues to Symbolic Intent (Acts 9:22 and 26)'. *Biblica Romae* 71, 1990, pp. 63-72. I have been helped considerably by this interesting article.
11. I owe this anecdote, which is typical of many, to Bill Fine of

AbilityNet, PO Box 94, Warwick, Warwickshire CV34 5WS. AbilityNet offers assistance to disabled people through the use of computers.

Chapter 3

12. Jane Wallman, 'Disability as Hermeneutic: Toward a Theology of Community', unpublished PhD thesis, University of Birmingham School of Education 2000.

Chapter 4

13. 'The presentation of the blindness of the disciples runs through the Gospel, but is particularly focused around chapter 8.22–26 ... so Mark is confident that the blurred spiritual vision of his church will be corrected.' E. S. Johnson, 'Mark VIII, 22–26: The Blind Man from Bethsaida', *New Testament Studies* 25, pp. 379f.
14. Sometimes printed as chapter 6 of Baruch.

Chapter 6

15. *Poems of Gerard Manley Hopkins*, ed. Robert Bridges, London: Oxford University Press 1956, p. 55 (from 'The Wreck of the Deutschland').
16. Papias, as reported by Eusebius, *Ecclesiastical History*, Book III, Ch. xxxix (tr. Kirsopp Lake, Vol. 1, London: Heinemann 1926, p. 293).

Index of Biblical Passages

The Old Testament

CPSIA information can be obtained
at www.ICGtesting.com
Printed in the USA
LVOW11s0426090618
580191LV00001B/1/P